DEAFNESS AND ETHNICITY

Services, policy and politics

Waqar Ahmad, Aliya Darr, Lesley Jones and
Gohar Nisar

First published in Great Britain in 1998 by

The Policy Press
University of Bristol
Rodney Lodge
Grange Road
Bristol BS8 4EA
UK
Tel no +44 (0)117 973 8797
Fax no +44 (0)117 973 7308
E-mail tpp@bristol.ac.uk
http://www.bristol.ac.uk/Publications/TPP/

In association with the Joseph Rowntree Foundation

© The Policy Press and the Joseph Rowntree Foundation, 1998

ISBN 1 86134 088 5

Waqar Ahmad is the Director of the Ethnicity and Social Policy Research Unit (ESPR), University of Bradford. **Aliya Darr** was a Research Fellow at ESPR, and is now at the School of Health Studies, University of Bradford. **Lesley Jones** was a Research Fellow at the Social Policy Research Unit, University of York, and is now a Senior Research Fellow at ESPR, University of Bradford. **Gohar Nisar** was a consultant to the project and now works for Bradford Metropolitan Council.

The **Joseph Rowntree Foundation** has supported this project as part of its programme of research and innovative development projects, which it hopes will be of value to policy makers and practitioners. The facts presented and the views expressed in this report, however, are those of the authors and not necessarily those of the Foundation.

Cover design by Qube Design Associates, Bristol.
Printed in Great Britain by Ashford Press, Southampton.

Contents

Acknowledgements

Our greatest debt is to the many deaf and hearing respondents who offered encouragement, were generous with their time and frank in discussion. Without their generosity and interest this text would not exist.

This report results from a joint project between the Ethnicity and Social Policy Research Unit (ESPR), University of Bradford and the Social Policy Research Unit (SPRU), University of York. A number of people have given help with this work. Sally Baldwin and Hazel Qureshi (SPRU, University of York) gave encouragement to pursue this research. At various times, Sally Pulleyn, Teresa Anderson, Jenny Bowes (SPRU) and Allison Campbell (ESPR) have given invaluable secretarial support. Alex O'Neil and Linda Ward of the Joseph Rowntree Foundation were encouraging and supportive. Rachel Bastikar gave excellent leadership to the Project Advisory Committee. We benefited from the guidance and facilitative role of all the committee members: Kevin Buckle, Sabina Chowdry, Jamil Iqbal, Shafiat Islam, Donna Jackman-Wilson, Kavita Kohli, Paul Lynch, Rukhsana Mehrali, Sarla Meisuria, Rita Mistry, Alex O'Neil and Mohammed Sayed. The sign language interpreters – Margaret Bairstow, Sheila Caley, Hannah Wyon, Harjit Phull and Mavis Rhodes – ensured effective communication during committee meetings. Sherrie Eugene facilitated and interpreted during interviews, as did a number of other interviewers. Brenda Mackay helped with translation of British Sign Language into English from videotaped responses. The audio-visual staff at the University of York helped with video-recording and salvaging virtually inaudible audio tapes. Our colleagues Karl Atkin and Rampaul Chamba provided intellectual and practical support. Charles Husband, Alex O'Neil, Dawn Pudney of The Policy Press and three anonymous reviewers provided helpful comments on the text.

We have benefited greatly from the involvement of all these people and acknowledge their support with pleasure and grateful thanks.

Waqar Ahmad, Aliya Darr,
Lesley Jones and Gohar Nisar

CHAPTER 1

Introduction

In Britain, minority ethnic communities have been extensively studied. In addition to the extensive literature on 'race' and 'ethnic relations', policy and practice have received considerable attention in recent years. Alongside this social scientific enterprise, epidemiologists and health service professionals have investigated ethnic inequalities in health status and healthcare. However, despite this considerable interest in minority ethnic communities, major gaps in knowledge remain. Some have argued that the research enterprise reflects the interests of the researchers better than it represents the needs of the minority ethnic groups (see Bhopal, 1992). Equally, others have criticised the narrow definitions of culture and the ethnic determinism of some policy research (Ahmad, 1993). Among the major gaps in research is knowledge on chronic illness, family-based care and physical and sensory disabilities in relation to minority ethnic groups.

The limited literature on deafness reflects the pattern observed in research on ethnicity and health: a concentration on epidemiological investigations and on children, with relatively little focus on social aspects of deafness or the experiences of older deaf people (we review this literature in Chapter 3). Deafness as an area of scholarly study and debate has rarely included minority ethnic deaf people. In particular, minority ethnic deaf people's or their families' experiences and perspectives are not well documented. Nor do we know much about how services are responding to minority ethnic deaf people's needs. This report is an attempt to chart the developments in the field of ethnicity and deafness in Britain, largely from the perspectives of minority ethnic deaf people themselves. The evidence is based on a study of initiatives across Britain. The findings are set in the wider context of literature on ethnicity and service provision.

In giving an overview of the wider debates in relation to ethnicity and services, and of deaf politics and policy, Chapters 2 and 3 provide the necessary context for understanding developments in ethnicity and deafness. The literature on ethnicity and services is vast, and Chapter 2 is necessarily selective in focusing on those debates relating to developments discussed here. Among these are issues around identity politics, the nature of specialist provision and its problems, and some speculative discussion of how minority ethnic parents may perceive 'Deaf culture' as no more than an extension of 'white culture'. Chapter 3 provides a rapid overview of the changing scene around both the construction of deafness and the relationship of Deaf people with hearing people and the state. The journey from the medical model of deafness to a model in which Deaf people see themselves as a linguistic minority oppressed by a hearing world's dependence on the spoken word, is accompanied by the increasing politicisation of Deaf people. However, Deaf people are far from homogenous in terms of perspective or need and this chapter explores the implications of this diversity (see note on terminology below). Chapter 3 also provides a brief review of literature on minority ethnic deaf people.

Chapters 4 to 8 are based on our research work (see the Appendix for a brief description of methods). Chapter 4 provides a national overview of initiatives involving minority ethnic deaf people. Based on a national postal and telephone survey, this is a precursor to what follows in greater depth in Chapters 5 to 8. Here, we discuss the main developments and the forces behind them, the diversity of action, the geographical and ethnic concentration of initiatives, the reproduction or continuation of the culture of special needs and, perhaps most importantly, how minority ethnic deaf people are reappropriating, cultivating and celebrating ethnic, religious and gender identities while retaining deafness as an important signifier of their personhood. Details of specific projects can be found in a directory published separately (Darr et al, 1997).

Chapters 5 to 8 are based on detailed face-to-face interviews with a range of people. A considerable amount of the activity identified was around user-led and socially and culturally oriented initiatives. Many focused around ethnic, cultural and religious identity – religious education, learning about cultural values and practices, celebrating functions and socialising. In some ways this represented a rediscovery of identities denied to young Deaf people partly because of their immersion into the ('white') Deaf culture and the English language. However, on the whole the celebration of new identities went hand in hand with a maintenance of their identity as Deaf people. These issues are explored in Chapter 5.

One major problem confronted by deaf people and their families concerns communication and language choice. Limited communication between deaf children and hearing parents makes conventional parent–child exchanges difficult; in addition, spoken home language, while acting as an important conduit for family and community membership, marginalises the deaf child who does not use speech in those cases where parents and family members do not use sign language. Chapter 6 explores these problems and developments from the perspectives of both deaf people and parents of deaf children. Parents, however, are far from passive or unconcerned; the chapter discusses a variety of activity around parents' sign language learning and deaf awareness. These initiatives also provide important access to information, networking and social support.

Chapters 7 and 8 explore issues in developing services for minority ethnic deaf people. Chapter 7 explores a number of interrelated concerns: communication difficulties in accessing services; attempts to make services more culturally sensitive; funding mechanisms and their relationship to service development, user involvement and accountability; and developments in the voluntary sector. These issues, however, are not unique to services for deaf people, as is introduced in Chapter 7 and further explored in Chapter 9.

Chapter 8, the last empirically based chapter, extends the discussion in addressing issues confronting workers such as training, networking and the different experiences of deaf and hearing workers. It also explores factors which help to make services user-friendly and the support needs of individual minority ethnic workers, often operating in hostile environments. Once again, issues raised here represent well-recognised difficulties in developing services for minority ethnic communities more generally.

Finally, Chapter 9 draws together the various themes and issues to emerge from this research and locates these within the wider literature on ethnicity, identity and services.

A note on terminology

It is important to make clear how the words deaf/Deaf are used in this report. The word 'deaf' (lower case) is used as a generic term to describe people with different forms of deafness. This book is about all deaf people.

The terms 'Deaf' (with a capital D), hard of hearing, deafened, deaf-blind, partially deaf/hearing and deaf (lower case) describe some of the diversity among deaf people. Deaf (with a capital D) is used in the way described by Padden and Humphries (1988) as a self-definition based on the use of sign language and membership of the 'Deaf community' and recognition of 'Deaf culture'. There is a more detailed discussion of the language used to describe deaf people in Chapter 3.

It is not an ideal system and at times it appears confusing but we follow this commonly used convention to differentiate between different deaf groups.

CHAPTER 2

Ethnicity, diversity and social welfare: the service context of minority ethnic deaf people

This chapter provides the necessary overview of debates around ethnicity and social welfare, including the role of identity politics in constructing community and individual needs and the responses from both the statutory and the voluntary sectors. The potential literature to review is vast and we have been selective in focusing on those issues and debates which are important in contextualising the research discussed in this report.

One important area of relevant literature, not discussed in detail, covers minority ethnic communities' knowledge of and access to welfare services. The findings can be quickly summarised. Numerous studies show minority ethnic users to be less well informed than the general population about a range of social welfare benefits (Craig and Rai, 1996; Ahmad and Walker, 1997; Atkin et al, 1997). Access to information and citizenship rights remains poor and users whose first language is not English continue to rely on relatives and friends for interpretation or are offered limited and often unsatisfactory interpretation support. Access to a range of services is clearly a problem. The inverse care law which operates in health and other services (that is, those in most need of services are least likely to receive these because better services tend to be located in more affluent areas) impacts more severely on sections of the minority ethnic communities who are more likely to be confined to inner-city residence and areas of industrial decline. Racist stereotypes held by professionals and institutional racism further hamper access to services across the board. Detailed discussion of these issues can be found in Ahmad and Atkin (1996a; 1996b), Atkin and Rollings (1993) and in other texts. And although not discussed in detail here, these facts of minority ethnic people's lives are important to bear in mind in reading this text.

This chapter deals with important issues necessary to understanding developments in the field of ethnicity and deafness. First, the nature and politics of racism, culture and identity are significant for any meaningful discussion of welfare provision to minority ethnic groups. Racism is increasingly articulated through the language of culture and politics of identity, where complex identities reduced to simplistic 'race' stereotypes are central to the increasingly narrow conceptions of belonging, deservingness and citizenship in which English ethnicity is taken as the norm. Second, a common feature in both ethnicity and deafness is identity, its construction, negotiation, maintenance and reproduction. Some of the important issues in identity construction and reproduction are addressed in the second part of this chapter. Third, identity politics has important implications for both the articulation of needs and the delivery of services. This is discussed in relation to the emergence of the minority ethnic voluntary sector in Britain. Finally, we bring together some of these themes in a speculative discussion of the similarities and differences between older and younger deaf people from minority ethnic groups around the intersections of ethnic/religious and deaf identity politics.

Culture, racism and identity politics

'Racism' is an elusive concept with competing definitions and conceptions across time, and across disciplines and political persuasions. Part of the confusion also rests in the fact that the term 'racism' encompasses attitudes, behaviour and outcome. 'Scientific racism', based on notions of the inherent superiority of some 'races' over others, so important in the legitimisation of slavery and imperialism, is now largely discredited in biological and social sciences alike. A popular and resilient definition of racism rested on psychological assumptions about an individual being racially prejudiced and having the power to exercise this prejudice to systematically disadvantage members of other racial groups. In its ability to locate the problem of racism in an individual's damaged psyche such a definition, reassuringly, absolves society and its institutions of responsibility. This psychological approach had great salience in British social policy in the shape of multiculturalism and, according to Mercer (1986, p 43) "is a central feature of the formation of discourses in education, social work, youth services, counselling, and personal social services...". By locating racism in damaged psyches and cultural difference, this approach articulates arguments for tolerance of difference through a better understanding of 'other cultures' rather than for equality of treatment, resources or outcomes, or for solutions aimed at an institutional level.

The late 1970s in Britain witnessed a major critique of the psychological and anthropological literature for such reductionist conceptions of racism and racialised representations of minority ethnic people's needs and behaviours. A new discourse emerged – becoming known as 'anti-racism' – which emphasised the importance of understanding and challenging the historical, ideological and institutional basis of racism. Racist behaviour and thinking, in this critique, was rooted in the history of slavery and imperialism, the ideology of white superiority over other 'races' and cultures, and the institutionalisation of such ideology in the workings of the state through its institutions (for example, CCCS, 1982). In terms of welfare, professional ideology was seen as a major vehicle for the articulation as well as legitimisation of racism. Ideologies turn racist ideas into received wisdom or common sense; professional ideologies give everyday common sense scientific legitimacy. Scully and Bart (1978) provide an account of this process in gynaecology textbooks, which both reflected contemporary societal views of women's role and sexuality and structured the medicalisation of womanhood. Similarly, Ahmad (1993) explores these issues in relation to racism in healthcare and research.

The concept of racialisation becomes important in the workings of institutional racism. 'Racialisation' is defined by Cashmore (1988, p 246) as the political and ideological process by which certain populations are identified by reference to their presumed physical characteristics, including behaviours, in such as way as to suggest that the population can only be understood as a supposedly biological entity. Increasingly culture – in its relation to lineage, history, common heritage and nation – has become the main vehicle for articulating racism in contemporary society (Husband, 1994). As Ahmad argues in relation to ethnicity, health and healthcare:

> **Racialization takes place in terms of notions of cultures being
> static and homogeneous and having a biological basis. This is
> then extended to notions of cultures having direct relationship
> to attitudes, expectations and behaviour. 'Cultures' here take
> on a rigid and constraining shape, rather than being nurturing
> and sustaining forces. These culturalist assumptions ignore
> issues of power, deprivation and racism. They result in culturalist
> explanations and feed into culturalist health policy options....
> (Ahmad, 1993, p 19)**

A particular example of racialisation is the medical discourse on consanguinity in explaining the higher rates of perinatal deaths and childhood disability in the Pakistani origin population compared to the white population (Ahmad, 1994). Whereas the data on infant mortality and congenital malformations, itself based on dubious categorisation, methods and interpretation, presents a picture of inconsistency and confusion this does not seem to affect the magical belief that consanguinity directly causes the predicament of the Pakistani population. The solution seems to rest, in this discourse, on changing marriage patterns and being more 'like us' – an approach which has a long history both in terms of ethnicity and health policy (witness the debates on eradicating vitamin D deficiency in Asians – Goel et al, 1981) and the health of poor people generally (Crawford, 1977). As Ahmad has argued:

> **The consanguinity hypothesis is over-simplistic to explain the higher rates of perinatal mortality and congenital malformations among the Pakistani population. Its popularity rests less on its scientific merit and more on its convenience in shifting the blame onto supposedly deviant cultures and marriage patterns and its fit with racist ideas of alienness and deviance. (Ahmad, 1994, p 423)**

Consanguinity is also increasingly indicted as the 'cause' of higher prevalence of deafness in Asian children and other disabilities such as thalassaemia (Ahmad et al, in press).

Anti-racism emphasised the role of institutions and ideology in the perpetuation of racism in society. Here racism is articulated through the routine workings of a racist society. An understanding of historical and contemporary relationships between developed and underdeveloped worlds and intersections of 'race' and class are vital in conceptualising racism. Combating racism is thus not about preaching tolerance or changing attitudes but about making changes in legal and institutional structures and practices.

Anti-racism privileged the shared experience of racism and discrimination of all non-white groups, leading to the adoption of 'black' as a symbol of political identity and the development of class-based alliances with other oppressed groups. It became popular with many left-wing councils in the 1980s. However, the late 1980s witnessed a notable backlash against anti-racism, and politically left-wing boroughs generally, from a hostile right-wing government, alongside criticisms from sections of and writers from the minority ethnic communities who felt that the level at which anti-racism functioned undermined cultural and religious values (Gilroy, 1990; Modood, 1988). Many in the Muslim communities, for example, found anti-racism largely irrelevant to their struggles for religious dignity and equality (Akhtar, 1989).

In terms of policy analysis the dichotomy of an over-structural approach (anti-racism) and an over-cultural approach (multiculturalism) is unhelpful. It is clear that structures, institutions and socioeconomic location of individuals and groups are important to their life chances and interaction with the state and its institutions. For the minority populations then, their generally poor housing, higher rates of unemployment and access to relatively poor quality of healthcare are important considerations and impact on their life circumstances and health. But equally, the minority ethnic populations are more than the sum total of racisms they experience or survive. Cultural resources – religion, community institutions, families, links with kin abroad – are vital sources of strength and important to their survival and success. Such resources are argued by Bryan et al (1985) as vital to the survival and sanity of African people through the period of slavery and are important for survival in a racist environment today. To not acknowledge the practical as well the symbolic importance of cultural resources is in many ways to negate a vital aspect of human existence.

Cultural identity and cultural reproduction

Ideological, structural and personal factors are important in reproducing identities. The reproduction of culture does not constitute implanting the norms, behaviours and aspirations of one generation into the minds and hearts of the next; not that this in itself would be a simple task. Reproduction takes place within a dynamic space involving negotiation and engagement, encompassing conflicting values within the family, influences of the wider society, personal agendas of various actors, the role of the economy, legal frameworks and the impact of and resistance to a racialised external world. If debates about agency and structure in social change or continuity are complex, they are even more so for minorities who live within their own as well as the wider society's structures and institutions, and where there may be incompatibility between the values of the two or where structures may constrain the exercise of normative values. Three major forces in cultural retention are considered below.

First, the role played by the family in reproducing values and behaviours is regarded as vital. Anthias (1992) notes that the reproduction of cultural values of honour and shame, identity and religion, obligations and expectations, relations with kin and ethnic group, and gender roles including sexual morality are regarded as essential to family responsibility. Family-based socialisation serves the twin functions of imparting religious and cultural values and countering the presumed conflicting or corrupting influences of the wider society (Anwar, 1977; Afshar, 1994). Anwar and

Afshar emphasise the potential conflict between the (highly generalised) prized values of communality, interdependence and mutual obligations in the Asian community and those (feared as negative influences by Asian parents) of independence, relative permissiveness and the secular morality of the white society.

Second, minority ethnic religious and cultural institutions play a crucial role in cultural reproduction. These include religious organisations, ethnic media, weekend and evening schools for religious education or mother tongue teaching, community centres and other voluntary organisations, ethnic businesses and art and cultural organisations (Rex, 1991). As Joly (1987) notes, minority communities seek "to reproduce in the British context the social characteristics which used to shape their way of life" in the country of origin.

Third, concerns about the values and institutions of the wider society, as well as external hostility, reinforce strong and somewhat exclusive identities (or encapsulation) and proscribe adoption of other cultural norms. This is less true of the second generation, however, whose knowledge of the wider British society and the English language may potentially make such excursions easier. External hostility also fosters newer forms of identity formation and mobilisation, as around Islam or previously as around the political symbol 'black' (Samad, 1992). This encapsulation is sustained through ideological as well as institutional structures.

Identity politics has been particularly salient in terms of the presumed predicament of the 'second generation'. Images of cultural conflict between the first and second generation are common in academia, policy debates and in lay discourses. Here the well-recognised generational conflict present in all communities takes on a racialised role being represented as a struggle between a presumed Westernised and liberal younger generation and a fanatical and alien older generation. Nonetheless, there are both imagined as well as real axes of social change which concern people from minority ethnic communities.

Perceptions of new freedoms as threatening to the continuation of traditional cultural values – such as parental authority and obligations, possible changes in marriage choices, concerns about sexual permissiveness – are strongly held by the older generation of Asians while among the older African Caribbean population there are worries about the increasing Anglicisation of black youth and the loss of a 'black' identity (Modood et al, 1994). Parents attempt to counter the presumed negative influences of the wider society through a variety of means, as noted by one of Anwar's respondents two decades ago:

> ... if we teach them from the very beginning with good reasons,
> they will respect us and follow the cultural values without
> questioning. However, if we leave it too late, they learn
> independence and other rude things at school and it becomes
> difficult to counter these influences at a later age. (Anwar,
> 1977, p 59)

One particular area of interest has been the role of female employment in changing gender roles (Westwood and Bhachu, 1988). Whereas African Caribbean women have had a high rate of labour market participation, women's role in the formal economy among Asian communities has often been limited. This has changed, to an extent, in the last two decades, especially among Sikh and Hindu women. According to Bhachu (1988), this increased relative economic independence has afforded women the opportunity to renegotiate traditional gender-based obligations and hierarchies and has resulted in a move towards more egalitarian household roles. Women – mothers, sisters, wives and daughters – have been regarded as the major sources and sites of, and threats to, male honour, and thus have been variously protected, paraded and controlled (for example, see the anthology of Urdu poetry, edited by Ahmed, 1991). Their greater access to the labour market, to a lesser extent even access to state benefits or indeed what may be regarded as 'corrupting' influences of the wider society, may be seen by some as major threats to minority cultures and both male and female identity. Worse still, for minority ethnic communities, as women are regarded as the primary socialisation agents, their presumed corruption may thus be seen to put in doubt the cultural and religious survival of future generations.

Others, however, do not share Bhachu's conclusions regarding the impact of the labour market in changing gendered household relations (for example, see other contributions to Westwood and Bhachu, 1988, such as Westwood, Warrier). On the whole, there appears only limited evidence of major change across generations, or in terms of gender roles. Afshar (1994), for example, found a variety of views about gender and family roles in young Pakistani women and their mothers and grandmothers, which were characterised as much by educational, class, denominational and other personal factors as by age. Drury's (1991) study of cultural change in Sikh girls supports this, showing that for these girls, identity was situational, varied and negotiated, in that some girls confined some Sikh traditions to specific contexts while others maintained them in all situations. In both cases, flexibility and compromise were more common responses of both young people and their parents than outright conflict. More recent work by Modood et al (1997) shows the process of social change to be variable between different ethnic and religious groups; for Asians, for example, somewhat greater change for Sikh and Hindu groups and more limited for Muslims. For the African Caribbeans, it appears more marked for men than women.

There is some evidence to suggest that social class and religious affiliation (and observance) are important influences on cultural identity. Qualitative as well as statistical data suggest that among the minority ethnic communities greater social and demographic change has occurred among the Indian and African Caribbean populations (whose migration to Britain took place earlier than for Pakistanis and Bangladeshis) compared to those of Pakistani and Bangladeshi origin (for example, Modood et al, 1994; 1997; CSO, 1996).

Identity politics and construction of needs

Whereas the state has manipulated identity politics by linking notions of citizenship and nationalism with racialised conceptions of identity, the minority communities have used notions of identity for a variety of struggles and forms of both inclusive and exclusive mobilisation. One area of particular importance is the way in which identity politics impinges on the construction of needs or delivery of services. Religion has occupied an ambivalent position in struggles for racial justice in Britain. This is not surprising in that common conceptions of and experience of lived religion cannot be separated from ideas about gender, social class and ethnicity. Akber Ahmed (1988) and Burghart (1987) note the difference between 'scriptural religion' and 'lived religion' – the latter cannot take place in a social or historical vacuum and other axes of identity politics impinge on people's lives; religious values are mediated by people's social and cultural contexts and biographies. That places of worship present a common front of oneness is itself an attempt at packaging religion for external presentation, as Burghart notes in the case of Hinduism in Britain. The diversity of fronts on which religious organisations can be divided is illustrated by the example of mosques and gurdwaras in Bradford where the axes of loyalty may include denomination, language, regional background and caste (see Singh, 1992 and Lewis, 1994 for discussion).

Whereas black churches may have played a stronger role in campaigning and service delivery, mosques, manders and gurdwaras have largely remained as places of worship. This is not to deny their social functions; that such institutions allow people of a given faith to come together in social exchange and foster common bonds is itself of great value. Many also have facilities for events such as weddings and meetings or provide 'langers' (free food distribution) on special occasions. But, with some exceptions, on the whole mosques, manders and gurdwaras have not become major sites for delivery of welfare services or campaigning on such issues. However, religiously based welfare centres and voluntary organisations have played a significant role in articulating and providing for welfare needs.

In recent years, however, the increasingly polarised politics of religious identity has impacted more strongly on people's perceptions of welfare needs. The anti-Rushdie demonstrations were organised on the basis of a Muslim identity, albeit those who took part in the demonstrations were predominantly south Asian Muslims, largely Pakistanis. Nor was religious devoutness a crucial factor in local Muslims feeling damaged by the Rushdie affair – pubs and clubs were as common as mosques for heated discussions about the need to struggle to preserve religious dignity. The response to the Rushdie affair arose amidst concerns that the major forms of political identity – secular and colour-based – were inappropriate for struggles around religious dignity and equality (Samad, 1992).

The feminist movement, at least in its early history, emphasised women's shared experience of sexual oppression above differences of social class, racial background or sexual orientation. The anti-racist movement, in the days of municipal socialism, was strongly aligned with the struggles around sexuality, gender and social class. Strategic identity constructions and alliances have a long history. But they also have their problems. Anti-racism is one example where a necessary political and intellectual project became much maligned by those on the right for its presumed excesses while at the same time being criticised from within for its rigidity, orthodoxy and refusal to accept that other aspects of personal or group identity (culture, religion) were legitimate bases for political organisation, defining needs or action (Gilroy, 1990; Modood, 1988). Such notions of identity have impacted on community constructions of needs and the ways in which services, including those within the minority ethnic voluntary sector, have developed.

The state has had a vested interest in managing diversity and constructing 'approved' group identities, partly through establishing official categories of ethnic groups (thus privileging ethnicity over other aspects of identity) as well as through grants and special projects, access to which is controlled through communities fitting into the state criteria of 'ethnically specific need'. Such constructions do matter in that they control the rules of engagement as well as creating a more palatable minority ethnic leadership – these leaders may well be 'radical' but within the boundaries of 'acceptable radicalism' defined by the state. 'Special' funding mechanisms through Section 11 of the 1966 Local Government Act (now subsumed under the Single Regeneration Budget) as well as other sources have acted as major vehicles for cultivating approved ethnic identities and palatable leaderships. The impact of state policy on constructing 'fictive unities' ('Pakistanis', 'Indians', etc) has been discussed by various writers (Ahmad, in press; Anthias and Yuval-Davis, 1993; Werbner, 1991; and at local service level, Imtiaz and Johnson, 1993). Such fictive unities then become important in terms of both construction of needs, lines of competition and struggles over resources. And as state privileges ethnicity over other forms of identity, fictive unities are constructed in terms of specific ethnic or cultural needs, distinct from those of other ethnic communities for whom similar services may already be being provided.

The politics of identity, then, has both empowering and oppressive consequences. Nor are we claiming that individuals or groups do not entertain more than one identity at a given time. At a positive level it allows for community cohesion, identification of common goals and necessary alliances and struggles to win concessions and obtain rights. It can be, and often is, a powerful tool for empowered self-organisation, increased self-worth and appropriate forms of resistance. But its oppressive side cannot be ignored.

First, a form of identity politics is very much the stuff of new racism and racialised nationalism where notions of identity can be used to deny people citizenship rights (see Ahmad and Husband, 1993). Second, it often leads to fragmentation of other forms of unity or to struggles whose rules have been established by outsiders, as in competition for resources from the local and central state for 'ethnic specific' needs. And as identities are often contested, and different people may give different aspects of their lives different importance, identity politics can encompass friction and conflict. An example of this is the relationship between the British disability movement and minority ethnic disabled people. The political disability movement gives great importance to unity in struggles. Commonality of experience of disablism is privileged over differences in gender, ethnicity, sexuality, etc – in other words disabled identity is regarded as the primary form of political identity for disabled people. Although some minority ethnic disabled writers have been influential in the British disability movement (for example, Stuart, 1994; Begum, 1994), a recent collection of writings by minority ethnic disabled people is highly critical of what they believe to be racist marginalisation from within the disability movement (Begum et al, 1994). The late Millicent Hill, in the same collection, advises black disabled people to turn to the black voluntary sector for support rather than the white disability movement (Hill, 1994). Clearly, for many contributors to that volume, their racial minority status is as or more important an aspect of their selfhood as their disability.

Ethnicity, social policy and the voluntary sector

Social policy in relation to minority ethnic communities has undergone numerous changes. Initial assumptions of eventual assimilation were short-lived and it was soon realised that the state had to act to facilitate the integration of migrant communities, in a Britain conceptualised as a pluralist society made up of different but notionally equal groups. (We have argued earlier that this conception is undermined by other discourses which define citizenship in relation to racialised conceptions of belonging.)

Successive governments of different political persuasions continue to believe there to be a trade-off between immigration controls and integration, with the latter considered to be impossible without the former. Further, increased understanding of each others' cultures was regarded as a necessary precursor to successful integration, based on assumptions that much strife is located in ignorance and that knowledge of other cultures engenders tolerance. Multiculturalism, as formal policy, espoused these ideals and an understanding of cultural backgrounds of minority ethnic communities became regarded as the key to appropriate service provision. This essentially reductionist approach led to the problems of minority ethnic communities being increasingly located in their 'cultural difference' and to the perverse conclusion that to improve their lot they must become more 'like us'. Critiques of this approach are available elsewhere (Pearson, 1986; Rocheron, 1988; Ahmad, 1994) and are not rehearsed here. The shift in policy to anti-racism, which resulted from a robust critique of multiculturalism as discussed above, has had a mixed and uneven history. It was espoused, to varying degrees and with different definitions, in social services and education, but made very limited inroads into the delivery of health services, social security or the white voluntary sector.

The emergence of the minority ethnic voluntary sector is inextricably related to both identity politics and the failure both of the formal welfare and the white voluntary sectors to cater for the needs of minority ethnic communities. Rex (1991) notes that minority voluntary organisations emerged very soon after the large-scale migration of the 1960s. Such organisations were also encouraged by the state as an efficient and cheap means of providing services. The construction of minority needs in terms of cultural difference gave further impetus to separate provision, this time through statutory sector funded 'special projects' aimed at meeting needs which were defined in terms of cultural specificity. Examples include campaigns around birth control, childrearing practices, pregnancy and vitamin D deficiency. 'Special projects' had many 'advantages' for the statutory sector. By locating the minorities' needs in their own presumed cultural deviance the statutory sector could absolve itself of any responsibility to change. Second, the provision of separate services was both considerably cheaper and a much more high-profile option. The authority could be seen to be taking action at little cost and with little 'disruption' to mainstream services. Third, through such initiatives the state created a tier of black professionals who were often willing to pursue the official agendas on behalf of state agencies.

Wholesale condemnation of such 'specialist provision', however, would be unfair. Even within the considerable restrictions of funding, narrow remit and short-termism, innovative and valuable work has been done in many initiatives – but often at the expense of the statutory sector remaining impervious to the need for change and at considerable personal cost to minority ethnic workers (Jeyasingham, 1992; Watters, 1996).

The voluntary sector, too, has had an ambivalent relationship with minority ethnic communities. Rooney and McKain (1990) argue that the white voluntary sector remains ill-equipped both in will-power and in resources and skills, to cater for the needs of minority ethnic groups, although some individual organisations have made significant efforts to become accessible to all sections of British society. This more progressive part of the white voluntary sector includes some deaf organisations.

One important reason for the development of the minority ethnic voluntary sector is the relative failure of the formal and white voluntary sectors to cater for minority ethnic groups. For example, in relation to healthcare McNaught (1987, p 21) argues that by organising an independent voluntary sector the minority communities are "voicing their dissatisfaction with the health service, responding to gaps in services, trying to meet the need for mutual support, and exploring alternative models and approaches to health care provision". Jeyasingham (1992) notes a number of different forms of initiatives in the area of community health: self-help groups; advocacy and interpreting projects; health-related tasks undertaken by organisations with wider remits, such as 'race equality councils'; resources and information projects; initiatives which focus on specific issues or conditions; community-based initiatives undertaken by professionals from statutory agencies; and neighbourhood-based community health projects. Other areas of considerable minority ethnic voluntary sector activity include mental health and housing (Watters, 1996; also see overview by Atkin, 1996).

Jeyasingham (1992), Saggar-Malik (1984) and Watters (1996) note the problems facing such initiatives. First, many such projects provide information and advocacy to their users. Yet, often the help their users need is in challenging the very agencies by whom the voluntary project is funded. This creates a dilemma for the voluntary agency, dissatisfaction for the user, and can lead to funding difficulties. Second, projects established with a limited brief and focusing on a particular community often become burdened by additional demands which they find difficult to reject or satisfactorily handle. The demands overstretch such projects and jeopardise their ability to fulfil those functions upon which they will be evaluated. Third, as Watters notes, the purchaser–provider split creates tensions for the minority ethnic voluntary sector. Many of the traditional tasks of such groups would encompass advocacy including campaigning in terms of unmet needs but this may well be regarded as part of the purchaser responsibility and therefore inappropriate for a small voluntary sector provider.

Finally, the reforms in the NHS and local government of the early 1990s have lead to the perversity of the minority ethnic voluntary sector often having to join with larger white voluntary organisations in order to compete for business in the provider market. This compromises the very values – small size, accessibility, flexibility, informal setting – which the black voluntary sector cherished, and necessitates alliances with the white voluntary sector whose failure to meet minority needs was partially responsible for the very emergence of the minority ethnic voluntary sector. The 1997 NHS White Paper is unlikely to significantly alter these structures and relationships.

Culture, identity and deafness

That there is a greater prevalence of deafness among certain minority ethnic communities is now well recognised by professionals, although statistical data remain limited (see Chapter 3). For example, sections of the Asian community, particularly Pakistanis, show higher rates of deafness at or soon after birth compared with the general population. Deafness raises a number of issues for people from minority ethnic groups and Chapter 3 provides a discussion of some of these. Here we discuss some potentially important differences between the first generation and second and subsequent generations in terms of deafness and its implications. In the absence of data on these issues, our discussion constitutes intelligent speculation based on knowledge of migration history and the process of continuity and change in minority ethnic communities.

It is generally accepted that migrants do not constitute a representative cross-section of the sending society. Selection biases in terms of age, gender, disability or general fitness may be present. For example, Odegaard (1932) explained the poorer mental health of Scandinavian migrants to America in terms of a negative selection bias – that is, that those who were psychologically 'less fit' were more likely to have migrated to make a fresh start. In the 1970s the more positive mental health status of south Asian migrants in Britain was attributed to possible positive selection bias – that the investment requirement to finance someone's passage was such that only the psychologically stable would be deemed worthy of such investment. What is clear in terms of the migration of minority ethnic groups in the 1960s is that they were largely composed of young working age men and, in the case of African Caribbeans, women. The physically impaired (including deaf) people, elderly people and the very young would have found it difficult to meet the rigid recruitment demands for a 'young, fit and flexible labour force'. Profound deafness in the first generation migrants in Britain is therefore likely to be relatively rare. (We recognise the argument for considering deaf people as a linguistic minority. However, in terms of industrial employment, deafness was and is still regarded as an 'impairment'.)

As acquired deafness is associated with, among other things, industrial noise and lower social class it may be that because of the almost exclusive concentration of some minority ethnic groups in heavy industry, textiles and other noisy work environments, acquired deafness among such groups would be at least as, if not more, common as in the general population. However, the responses of adults with acquired deafness may be fundamentally different to those who are deaf from birth. Their notions of self and location in terms of specific cultural/ethnic/religious/linguistic identities would be firmly established before deafness occurred. The shared deafness which they have in common with other deaf adults may be an insufficiently strong bond for unity against differences of culture, language and religion. At a speculative level, we would expect older minority ethnic people with acquired deafness to be integrated within their own ethnic communities and not to have a particularly strong notion of having a 'deaf identity'. Certainly the personal experience of those of us who are from the Asian community is that becoming hard of hearing is regarded very much as part of becoming old – something one has to accept as natural and to cope with, either with or without professional intervention. 'Deaf culture', for these older deaf people as well as by minority ethnic groups generally, may well be regarded as no more than an extension of 'white culture', something which offers little attraction but many potential threats, and therefore is not for them.

A major consequence of the relative lack of first generation deaf migrants is that young deaf people from minority ethnic communities have few deaf role models from their own ethnic/religious community in Britain. This may create difficulties both for them and their families, and not having the same-culture role models may make challenges to Western notions of deaf identity more difficult.

Second generation deaf people

Sociologists and anthropologists problematise the term 'second generation'. They argue that the term represents an amalgam of age and migration status in suggesting that second generation are the children of migrants whereas the reality is more complex. The history of migration is such that, alongside children being born in Britain in the 1970s and later, there has been a progressively reduced but sizeable inflow of dependent children and families from the settlers' countries of origin. Many of the relatively young 'second generation' may themselves, therefore, be migrants into Britain. This, however, is not a major issue for our discussion (see Shaw, 1988).

Issues of identity in relation to the second generation minority groups have had a high profile both in academia and in the popular media, as discussed earlier. They also cause concern for parents of these second generation young people as discussed above. Many of these arguments are relevant here, but we will concentrate specifically on issues of identity and deafness, and some of the ways in which the younger deaf people may be different from first generation deaf people in terms of expectations, aspirations, networks and involvement in Deaf culture.

A variety of influences impinge on the development of personal and group identities, as discussed above. Apart from family, religious and cultural institutions and the media – this is in no way an exhaustive or extensive list – the role of professionals is important in the development of the self. The importance of the so-called 'psy(chology) complex' in the lives of children is well recognised. This 'psychologisation' allows childhood to be made an important site of state intervention through the workings of a range of professionals such as health visitors, social workers, teachers and psychologists. Many of these influences are ideological, and are accepted as normal or in the best interests of the child. Others are sanctions legally imposed on children or their parents on behalf of the state. In addition to the above, the role of a range of professionals involved in deaf services assumes great importance in the lives of deaf children and their parents, including those from minority ethnic communities.

Through the involvement of these professionals, parents of deaf young people will inevitably be steered not just towards appropriate services (as defined by professionals) but will also be presented with appropriate ideological fixes. Choices for parents may include those between sign language and oralism (and within oralism, between English and the child's family language) and involvement in deaf activities and events to allow their child access to peers and role models (for discussion see Chamba et al, in press). The lack of availability of services such as speech therapy in languages other than English will dictate in favour of English as the main spoken language. Alongside making access to educational and social facilities easier, it also influences what sort of educational and social facilities are accessible. The favouring of the English language will also be influenced by ideas about 'linguistic confusion' resulting from a deaf child using two spoken languages.

Although reproduction of culture is complex, two important elements in it are the preservance of an individual's own cultural and religious values through experience, instruction and involvement in family and social institutions, and families' attempt to guard against what they regard as harmful external influences, as already discussed. Mother tongue teaching, ethnic entertainment, religious education, establishment of places of worship are all attempts by minority communities to create those institutions which enable the reproduction and maintenance of cherished cultural values and practices. The deaf child's immersion into sign language and white Deaf culture, loss of development of mother tongue (in favour of English or exclusive reliance on sign language), lack of culturally appropriate signs for many religious events, and relatively little use of sign language by hearing parents, would all make their access to these vital socialising institutions difficult if not impossible. Parents of deaf children may end up with fewer resources for cultural socialisation of their deaf child and to deal with a greater degree of external influences they find difficult to challenge. Deaf culture and its associated facets and services may then be regarded by minority ethnic deaf young people and their parents with extreme ambivalence: at the same time empowering them in relation to the hearing world but compromising their ethnic and religious heritage; giving access to education and social opportunities but possibly alienating them from their hearing ethnic group peers or elders. Our personal experience of parents of deaf children would bear this out and research information supporting this is becoming available (Chamba et al, 1998). Some of these issues are explored in later parts of this report. These issues, though uncomfortable to consider, are important to discuss and have a profound impact on the minority ethnic deaf person's identity.

Conclusion

We have discussed the necessary context for understanding the lives of deaf people from minority ethnic communities. The problems of inadequate information about welfare, the poor quality and inaccessibility of services and negative attitudes of service providers, which affect members of minority ethnic communities generally, will have an even greater impact on the lives of minority ethnic deaf people. We have argued that it is important to understand identity politics as a necessary context for understanding minority ethnic deaf initiatives. Parallels can be drawn with other issues, such as ethnicity and disability, where the privileging of one identity (say disability) may be felt to marginalise other identity claims (say ethnicity). Although identities tend to be negotiated, flexible and situational, construction of needs on the basis of a single or dominant identity (for example, Deaf culture) takes on a rigid form which does not always allow for alternative approaches or challenges to dominant norms. Equally important in understanding the situation of young deaf people from minority ethnic groups are the processes of cultural reproduction and social change. Identity politics, as well as the failure of both the statutory and the white voluntary sectors, also have important bearings on the development of the minority ethnic voluntary sector. Finally, we have discussed similarities and differences between minority ethnic people with acquired deafness and people who are born deaf or are deaf from an early age. We argue that the consequences for ethnic and religious identity formation for these groups will be very different both for the deaf person and their families.

Chapter 3 provides an overview of debates in deafness, including the organisation of deaf services.

Perspectives on deafness: politics and policy

This chapter looks at the culture, community, language and politics of deafness. It also examines the medicalisation of service provision, the language and politics of defining, describing and measuring deafness and the ways in which deafness is represented in the media. We trace the widely different experiences of being deaf and the changes in service delivery to deaf people. Deaf people are subjected to surveillance and monitoring by a range of professionals, especially in early life and at school. Part of the disablism that Deaf people who use sign language experience, rests on the belief that the spoken word is superior to sign language; a belief reflected in the rise of, and supported by, the 'audist' professionals (see Corker, 1994; Lane, 1993). This chapter provides a necessary, if rapid, overview of these debates. In the final section, we provide a brief overview of the limited literature on ethnicity and deafness.

Numbers

The numbers of deaf people (using the term generally to cover the whole range of deafness) are notoriously difficult to estimate accurately. Between 17% and 25% of the British population are estimated to have a "significant hearing loss" (Davies, 1987; OPCS, 1985). There is a wide spectrum of deafness variously experienced and defined, as illustrated by the following facts:

- one in a thousand people is born deaf;
- the majority of people over 70 have difficulty in hearing;
- 50,000 people use British Sign Language;
- deafness was the second most common disability in the OPCS (1985) Disability Survey;
- there are an estimated 21,000 deaf-blind people in the UK.

These figures may well be an underestimate and need to be treated with caution. Prevalence rates in minority ethnic communities are discussed in the final section of this chapter.

Deaf people are not all the same

The terms used to describe deaf people have been the subject of controversy and have been effectively 'reclaimed' from hearing professionals. Deaf people use different languages to communicate and choose different ways to describe themselves. 'Deaf', 'hard of hearing', 'deafened' and 'deaf-blind' constitute the main broad categories for describing deaf people. As noted in the introductory chapter, Deaf, with a capital 'D', refers to people who see themselves as part of the 'Deaf community', and regard British Sign Language as their first language (Padden and Humphries, 1988). Lane and Grodin (1997) go so far as to use DEAF to denote someone as part of the DEAF WORLD.

Deaf, with a lower case 'd', is used as a generic term to cover all people who experience deafness. It includes deaf people who use speech (sometimes referred to as 'oral deaf'), as well as hard of hearing, deafened and deaf-blind people. Hard of hearing people constitute the largest group. They usually have some hearing and probably have gradual, relatively mild deafness. They are more likely to be older (60% of those over 70 have marked deafness), to wear a hearing aid and to communicate by speech and lip reading. 'Deafened' is the term used to describe people who have become significantly deaf as adults. They usually prefer the spoken language and their degree of deafness is such that a hearing aid is of no use to them. They sometimes see themselves as different from Deaf people who use sign language, because they continue to use speech for communication. 'Hearing impaired' is sometimes used as an overall term about people with varying degrees of deafness. The term 'partially deaf' (or partially hearing) is sometimes used to describe people with some hearing who may use speech or sign language or both (as in sign-supported English). Finally, deaf-blind people include those with a wide range of deafness combined with different degrees of blindness. This means that some deaf-blind people use sign language (hands-on or within a restricted visual frame) and some use spoken language or the manual alphabet to spell out words on the hand.

As in many other areas, the language used to define deaf people is the subject of debate and the language choices made by different groups of deaf people have important implications. Some distinctions rest on the language or communication medium used by deaf people; others are based on medical definitions such as congenital and 'pre-lingual' deafness.

The medicalisation of deafness

Over the last century deafness has become medicalised and deaf people's behaviour has been pathologised. Medicalisation relates particularly to the definition, measurement and diagnosis of deafness. Deafness is measured through clinical or functional tests. The functional tests ask questions such as 'Can you hear someone whispering?' (Schein and Delk, 1974) whereas the clinical tests monitor decibels of hearing loss through audiological measurement. Noble (1991) and Beaudry and Hetu (1991) have pointed out the variation in audiological testing, suggesting it is not always the 'objective' measure it is thought to be. In contrast, functional tests allow input into assessment by the deaf person. On the whole, however, the 'measurement industry' has located deafness firmly in the medical discourse and medical settings, which also influences the public perceptions of deafness. For example, the diagnosis of a deaf child by health workers often leads parents to expect a 'medical outcome'. For many, this represents both oppression of deaf people by hearing professionals and by hearing people generally (Lane, 1993). In a Foucauldian sense such measurement and quantification represent the acceptable face of social control of the deaf by the hearing.

Diagnosis and 'treatment'

The diagnosis of deafness and its 'treatment', if any, is provided by medical staff – health visitors, general medical practitioners, ENT (ear, nose and throat) or audiological physicians, audiological scientists, physiological measurement technicians in audiology and hearing therapists. All these are medical or paramedical staff based in hospital or community health settings. This means that having a hearing aid fitted is not seen in the same way as having an eye test; the latter is now routinely available in shopping centres. One consequence of this medicalisation of deafness is that 'high-tech' solutions may be given a high profile: surgical intervention such as cochlear implants and even hearing aids themselves are examples of such high-tech fixes. Equally, the media remains obsessed with the 'bionic ear' (cochlear implant) and other 'cures' for deafness as an extension of their fascination with 'cyberbodies' (see Yardley, 1997).

In terms of 'prevention', there is considerable interest in genetics. The higher incidence of deafness in the Pakistani population, for example, is routinely offered as resulting from the practice of consanguineous marriage in the Pakistani population. As noted in the previous chapter, the medical fascination with consanguinity extends to other fields and is explored by Ahmad (1994). Lane (1993) points out that in some schools in Mexico parents of deaf children are required to sign an agreement to attend genetic counselling before a child will be registered in school.

Pathologising the behaviour of deaf people

Deaf people's behaviour is pathologised in a number of ways. There is an emphasis in the literature on the 'isolation', 'paranoia' and 'psychological effects' for people who are deafened later in life (Myklebust, 1960; Thomas and Herbst, 1980). Equally there is a tendency in the medical and educational literature to infantilise people who are born deaf (Hoffmeister, 1996) and to see them as immature and with no language skills. Lane (1993; 1995) describes as 'audism' the oppressive nature of measuring competence by spoken language and hearing skills. Hoffmeister (1996) analyses the affects of these processes on education for deaf children by looking at the language used in special education text books. He highlights the emphasis on 'correction and cure' for deafness, where the ear is seen as an organ that needs to be fixed. This is directly at odds with the 'cultural' view of deafness as he describes it. 'The mask of benevolence' is Lane's term (also the title of one of his books) for the paternalistic approach used by both medical and other professionals to "disable the deaf community" (Lane, 1993). Maggie Woolley (1987), director of a large arts organisation, writes about her experience, as a deafened person, of this medicalisation:

> Read any book on deafened people and the lack of self-confidence and poor self-image is discussed [it is] seen as a product of the inability to hear, of faults in the ears and not of a society which does not value us. We are stuck with these pathological models and medical definitions of who we are, when in reality we are not sick or ill people. We are people who are socially, psychologically and politically oppressed. (Woolley, 1987, pp 172-3)

A critique of oppression of deaf people by professionals, and by hearing people generally, is at the heart of the political view of deaf people and the Deaf community.

The culture of deafness

The diversity among deaf people needs to be recognised. The experiences, needs and political outlook of deaf people vary and increasingly the importance of gender, ethnicity, religion and sexuality is being recognised in sections of the Deaf community. Deaf culture itself is the subject of interest, debate and historical analysis (Padden and Humphries, 1988). Lane (1993) and Schein and Delk (1974) provide a demographic overview of deaf people in the US. Higgins takes this a stage further by describing deaf people as living "within a world which is not of their own making, but one which they must continually confront". He likens this chosen separateness or encapsulation as a response to 'handicapism' or 'deafism', and draws parallels with the African American people's response to racism — "the set of assumptions and practices which promote the differential and unequal treatment of people because of their deafness" (Higgins, 1988; see also Scott, 1981 in relation to blindness). Higgins points out that membership of the Deaf community is 'ascribed' rather than 'assigned' — steps have to be taken towards establishing a strong Deaf identity in order to acquire it. Membership of the Deaf community was described by Baker (1991) as being based on a complex combination of audiological, social, linguistic and political gateways.

Whereas the earlier assumptions about the Deaf community were inclusive of all deaf people, Woodward (1982) and Padden and Humphries (1988) noted in the 1980s that Deaf with a capital 'D' was generally used by people whose first language is sign language (for example, British Sign Language) and who see themselves as part of a distinct community with their own language and culture. Their preference is to be seen as a linguistic minority rather than a group of disabled people. The visual language and means of exchanging information used by Deaf people are important aspects of Deaf cultural norms. There is more eye contact and touching than hearing people use, which leads to Deaf people's stereotype of hearing people as avoiding their gaze and not liking to be touched. Deaf culture, language, identity and community are enmeshed (Becker, 1980; Padden and Humphries, 1988; Jones and Pullen, 1992). Deaf children in the past have mostly attended residential schools so that the culture is usually passed along 'horizontally' from other children in the same way that the language is through contemporaries at school or in Deaf clubs. The family is not usually the major arena for Deaf socialisation as about 89% of deaf children have hearing parents (see also Chapter 2). The 'stigma' of being deaf is often a cohesive factor and adds to the strong bonds between deaf children often growing up together in residential schools. Eighty-five per cent of Deaf people choose to marry other Deaf people.

Deaf drama and sign language history and storytelling have been vehicles for perpetuating Deaf culture. Oral history has a strong sign language equivalent in the Deaf heritage by means of which strong Deaf role models are presented which help create a sense of historical identity. There are also written Deaf histories, by Deaf authors, beginning to emerge (Grant, 1990;

Jackson, 1990). However, this deaf history is not without its problems. Padden and Humphries (1988) argue that Deaf heritage is about white deaf history and Holcombe and Wood (1989) point out that it excludes deaf women.

Lane (1993) argues that the history of deaf people is one of marginalisation and damaging perceptions held by hearing people. However, sign language and the increasing recognition of the Deaf community's own perspectives were changing these perceptions – in particular, Deaf people positioning themselves as a linguistic minority rather than a disabled group (see also Lane et al, 1996).

Deaf clubs have in the past been important in the development of Deaf culture. This is now changing as younger Deaf people tend not to be as involved as previous generations, for whom these clubs were the main focus of social life. Instead of being on committees of the local Deaf voluntary organisations, younger Deaf people tend to meet in pubs (BDA, 1994) or become involved in activities such as drama, sign singing, youth training or education courses. Membership of the Deaf community is important, however, and is still often seen as related to Deaf club attendance. This community includes 'honorary' members, such as the children of Deaf parents who have an identity as part of the Deaf world, and there is an organisation by the name of Children of Deaf Adults (CODA) which brings together children of Deaf parents (see Preston, 1995 for an account of this). Higgins (1988) writes of his own 'courtesy' membership, offered to 'wise' outsiders, but he stresses that this is only a partial membership – attendance at Deaf clubs is part of acquiring this honorary membership.

Deaf clubs have come to reflect British white Deaf culture. They revolve around social activity often accompanied by 'social drinking', despite historically being founded and run by Christian religious organisations. In some areas, the clubs are under pressure to change to reflect the religious and cultural sensitivities of their changing membership.

Deaf culture has been communicated largely through the teaching of British Sign Language (BSL) and 'Deaf awareness' courses to hearing people. This is rather different from the way that Deaf culture is acquired by Deaf people themselves, as discussed earlier. BSL teaching has had an enormous impact as a popular adult learning course (Jones, 1993). It is taught mostly by Deaf tutors to hearing people and it emphasises not just political debates but also relatively simple practical aspects of communication. Examples of the latter include learning to get a Deaf person's attention in a group by tapping one person and passing it on until the Deaf person is alerted by their immediate neighbour or by switching a light on and off in a room full of Deaf people to get their attention. 'Deaf awareness' courses for employers or people working with Deaf colleagues are also focused on language, communication and culture. Time is spent on learning language and communication skills but also learning to look people in the eye. This may be problematic for people in some cultures, however, where respect is indicated by not looking directly at someone.

Cultural cohesion and conflicts

Deaf culture is significant in building a cohesive Deaf identity although, as we will discuss, many deaf people may feel excluded from this collective identity. Like any other culture, it provides a shared history, a sense of belonging and rules for belonging. Young writes in the foreword to *Britain's deaf heritage* (1990, p 13): "Deaf heritage is important to deaf people. It is part of our culture but it is also an opportunity for hearing people to become aware of how rich deaf people's heritage truly is".

Linked with language, culture provides cohesion and a sense of pride particularly to people denied access to basic rights and responsibilities. Deaf culture is not always visible to the hearing world, as Preston notes in relation to having deaf parents:

> If I was Black or Italian or something people might understand they might say 'oh, your family's different because that's a different culture'. But when they look at me they just see this white guy who is too involved with his family – it just does not compute. (Preston, 1995, p 10)

Deaf culture, for some Deaf people, provides a strong argument for educational segregation where Deaf children are taught together, separately from hearing children, in anticipation that it will reinforce a positive sense of identity and pride. By the same token, integration in education is sometimes seen as eroding the language and culture of Deaf people (Ladd, 1991).

However, 'Deaf culture' has led to problems within the deaf world (Gregory and Hartley, 1991). Some 'cultural norms' have become *the* orthodoxies. Deaf people with a capital 'D' are sometimes seen as the 'real' deaf, who may be regarded as reflecting the views of all deaf people. This has led to an uneasy alliance between deafened, hard of hearing and oral deaf people when competing for resources. There has often been a tendency for service providers to think that putting in a sign language interpreter solves the problem of access to services for 'the deaf'. This non-recognition of diversity in deaf people, and the relative dominance of the Deaf group, means that the communication needs of someone with a hearing aid, who would usually follow speech with an inductive loop to amplify the sound, may be ignored. The same applies to note-takers or lip speakers who would be useful for profoundly deaf people who do not use sign language. This can cause tension between Deaf people who use sign language and deafened and hard of hearing people who do not.

The 'silent majority' of hard of hearing people usually do not identify themselves as deaf or part of the Deaf community (Jones and Pullen, 1989). However, for some hard of hearing people, the discovery of the Deaf culture and sign language is pleasing (see Woolley, 1987).

Deaf-blind people also have an uneasy place between the deaf, blind and hearing worlds, as do deaf people with other disabilities. And just as there is an uneasy alliance between different sections of the deaf community, the relationship between broadly defined deaf people and the political disability movement remains problematic.

Images of deafness

There has been an increasing interest in Deaf culture and in sign language in recent years. In literature there have been novels such as *The heart is a lonely hunter* by Carson McCullers with a central character who uses sign language or Eudora Welty's *The key*. In *The silent world of Nicholas Quinn*, a detective novel by Colin Dexter, the central character is deaf and lip reads, and this is used as a device to further the plot. Interestingly, Dexter, the creator of the British television detective series *Inspector Morse,* is himself deafened. He writes the deaf character in this novel as a man with a professional life even though his role is to be murdered because he can lip-read information to which he should not have had access. In Elizabeth George's *For the love of Elena*, the murdered person is deaf but is portrayed as intelligent and knowing.

There has also been film and television interest in deaf people, such as *Children of a lesser god*. First performed as a play in 1986, and later as a film, it describes a young deaf woman's struggle to find a language for herself and an identity in a relationship with a hearing man. The award-winning film *Love is never silent* is based on a novel about a deaf couple and their hearing daughter during the depression in America. The British comedian, actor and writer, John Cleese wrote a character based on his hard of hearing mother in the British television series *Fawlty Towers,* which presented a realistic view of a hard of hearing person fighting back at an inconsiderate hearing person who is made to look foolish for his poor communication skills.

Mostly though, deaf characters are portrayed as needy or naive. Shuchman (1991) notes that in film "a collective Hollywood is guilty of the perpetration of a pathological view of deafness as a disease and of deaf individuals as abnormal" (see also Grant, 1990; Hevey, 1993). Deaf people are also portrayed as being white. We know of no deaf character in mainstream English language film, television or literature who is from a minority ethnic community.

Specialist Deaf broadcasting has been significant in raising awareness about deaf issues. British television now has programmes aimed at deaf audiences such as *See hear* and *Sign on*, as well as sign language interpreting on some news coverage and subtitles on an increasing number of television programmes. The Queen's speech on Christmas Day is interpreted by a deaf interpreter, for example. Seeing competent and assertive deaf presenters has an impact on hearing people who might have a notion of deaf people as tragic figures.

Images of deafness in the media are accompanied by an increasing interest in Deaf culture through academic texts but also through drama, art, sign poetry and singing. Ladd (1991) calls this the 'Deaf revival'. There is now a bookshop in the Forest of Dean which specialises in books about deafness and, although most of the books are American, there is an increasing amount which are written by other nationals and by deaf people themselves (for example, Grant, 1987; 1990; Jackson, 1990). Both the general research and writing interest on deafness, and the course literature for the five universities (Durham, Bristol, Wolverhampton, Central Lancashire and the City University) which offer deaf studies, make this a growing area of study and scholarship in the UK; similar developments can be seen in the United States and Scandinavia.

Deafness and language

As noted, Deaf and hard of hearing people do not all use the same language: some use sign language (BSL in the UK), others use spoken languages or a combination of spoken and sign language. Speedy (1987) found that 47 spoken home languages other than English were used in the homes of deaf children; Punjabi, Urdu and Gujarati were the most commonly used apart from BSL.

Sign language

There has been a tremendous growth in the use of sign language as the preferred language of Deaf people in the last 30 years. This is reflected in scholarship (Stokoe, 1960; Kyle and Woll, 1985) and in the media (as already noted). Sign language has also been helped by the patronage of high profile people such as Diana, the late Princess of Wales, in her role as patron of the British Deaf Association. In written texts, the upsurge is evident in books by people such as Harlan Lane (1984; 1993; 1995) and Oliver Sacks (1989). Sacks' book about the Deaf President Now Campaign at Gallaudet University in Washington did a great deal to publicise not only sign language but also Deaf people's attempt to gain control over their own education. The students at Gallaudet University for Deaf People fought for a deaf president, H. King Jordon, after a hearing director who did not know any sign language was appointed. Lane (1993; 1995) has looked at sign language as part of a cultural phenomenon, as has Groce (1985) with her study of Martha's Vineyard, a community where sign language was routinely used by the large number of deaf and hearing people.

Historically, education of deaf children has been dominated by the battle between oralism and sign language. Oral education has dominated for most of the 20th century in the UK and elsewhere in Europe and it is interesting to note that sign language was banned at a convention of hearing teachers of deaf children held in Milan in 1880. Since the 1960s, however, sign language has increasingly been recognised as a language in its own right, not merely mime or gesture (Brennan et al, 1980; Kyle and Woll, 1985; and in the US, Stokoe, 1960). By the time of the publication of the first *Dictionary of British Sign Language* in 1992, there had been a move towards a bilingual (spoken and sign language) policy in some local education authorities. Elsewhere in Europe, sign language has gained state level recognition as a language; in Sweden sign language was officially recognised in 1983 and the European Union is proposing to do the same.

Language issues have particular implications for deaf people from minority ethnic communities where there is often more than one spoken language used at home. Trilingualism is effectively being used where, for example, sign language, an Asian language and English are the home languages. Parents of deaf children whose first language is not English have to consider, firstly, whether to educate their child in sign or spoken language and, secondly, which spoken language to use if that is their choice.

Newly arrived deaf people who use sign languages from countries such as Somalia and Bosnia are also confronted by the prospect of both a new spoken language and a new sign language to learn. There are regional dialects of sign language in addition to different sign languages in each country, as is shown by Christensen and Delgado (1993) in their study of deaf African Americans, American Indians, Hispanic and Asian/Pacific Islanders. Nuru (1993) also notes that black deaf children in the US switched codes between black and white signing at home and in school, as does Woodward (1982) for 'black' and 'white' southern US sign language users. Similar code switching has been seen among Hispanic deaf children in the US and among black and Asian deaf people in Britain.

Some signs which were perceived to be racist by non-white deaf people and their families have been changed; examples include the sign for Chinese people, previously shown by pulling the eyes to the side and now signified by a Mao jacket signed across the chest, and the sign for Russia being changed from the clenched fist to a beard being cut off.

Linguistic dominance

Language has strong links with knowledge and dominance. Here three types of linguistic dominance can be identified. First, as noted, spoken language has traditionally occupied the space of 'dominant' language against which sign language has struggled for acceptance. We have noted that the recognition of sign language constitutes a considerable victory for sign language users.

Second, in contemporary thinking on deafness, sign language is competing for equality with other choices of communication by deaf people. Although 50,000 Deaf people use BSL in Britain, there are greater numbers of deafened and hard of hearing people who use written and spoken languages. People who have some hearing or have become profoundly deaf later in life, or who have been educated using speech, often prefer to rely on lip reading, sign-supported English or writing things down. In Britain, BSL has become the recognisable symbol which represents the Deaf community and it has tended to be the dominant language within the social and political realms of deafness. There is some tension between sign language and speech users within the Deaf community (Higgins, 1988; Lane, 1993).

Finally, just as spoken languages such as English have become a symbol of Western power and dominance through their imposed association with progress and modernity, similar linguistic imperialism is sometimes apparent in the imposition of Western sign languages on deaf people of underdeveloped countries. An example of this is the use of American Sign Language with deaf children in some Kenyan schools rather than the development of indigenous sign language. A quite different aspect of this is that black deaf children in South Africa used sign language in schools during apartheid while 'white' deaf children were educated in the notionally superior medium of spoken language.

Access and interpreting

Language, both sign and spoken, also facilitates access to information, knowledge and resources. For different deaf people this may be possible through different means. However, any kind of 'interpreting' is a two-way process; it is necessary for both the deaf and hearing person and not just to solve the deaf person's 'problems' as it is sometimes described. The channel between two languages can go through the following people:

- sign language interpreters
- communicators
- lip speakers
- note-takers
- deaf-blind guide communicators
- computer-aided transcription operators, subtitlers, and machine shorthand writers.

Those most often seen are sign language interpreters. These are qualified interpreters who have passed examinations held by the Council for the Advancement of Communication with Deaf People (CACDP). In order to follow certain codes of practice, they should:

- be standing between two parties, representing neither;
- be functionally bilingual;
- work in real time (at the same time as speech);
- work from a 'source' language into a 'target language' conveying appropriate meaning and intent;
- be concerned with meaning and how this should be interpreted. (Kyle, 1991)

In 1992, the Commission of Enquiry into Human Aids to Communication recommended a structure for the use of only qualified or trainee interpreters. There are, in early 1998, approximately 130 qualified sign language interpreters working in Britain of whom, to our knowledge, only nine are from minority ethnic communities.

There are a number of issues about sign language interpreting that can limit access for those people working with interpreters, some of which are common to spoken language interpreting. First, confidentiality can be seen as problematic in a relatively small community, particularly when interpreters are adult children of Deaf parents. Second, the role of an interpreter needs to be distinguished from that of an advocate. In the case of Deaf people who use sign language, interpreting was previously often undertaken by social workers with deaf people, and the distinctions between interpreting and advocacy were blurred. This overlap is now seen as unacceptable. Third, interpreting by family or friends is often seen as the only option when there is no funding to pay interpreters or no qualified interpreters available. This causes problems when the 'interpreter' is too young or not knowledgeable enough to take on the responsibility. Sometimes confidentiality is not observed and roles become confused. These problems are all too familiar to members of hearing minority ethnic communities who routinely rely on family members for English-language interpreting (Ahmad and Walker, 1997). Fourth, interpreting between spoken English and sign language is much more common than that between other spoken languages (for example, Urdu, Punjabi, Cantonese) and sign language. There is a severe shortage of sign language interpreters with competence in languages other than English, which disadvantages non-English users.

Deaf people who do not use sign language rely on lip reading and clear speech from the person they are having a conversation with. Lip reading is obviously more difficult when there is more than one spoken language used and oral interpreting (or lip speaking) in languages other than English appears to have developed very little. Note-taking and computerised text services also remain underdeveloped and are English based.

Loop systems, computerised note-taking and subtitling on television, video and text telephones assist access to information, knowledge and resources, although English based. Baker (1991) comments on the distinction between technology that tries to 'normalise' deaf people (for example, hearing aids) and that which recognises the difference (for example, text telephones). Deaf people have also taken advantage of non-specialist technology, such as fax machines, electronic mail and computers.

The politics of deafness

Politically, Deaf people have maintained a relatively high profile over the past few years largely through taking control not only of their own lives but also the way in which they are represented. This is sometimes called the 'deaf construction' of deafness as opposed to the 'hearing construction' of deafness (Harris, 1995). A number of high profile and successful campaigns have been important in maintaining deafness on the political and public agenda (as has the presence of a deafened MP Jack [now Lord] Ashley). Some of these have been orchestrated by the, now defunct, political lobbying organisation for deaf people, Deaf Accord. One such campaign is the Deaf Broadcasting Campaign, begun by the National Union of the Deaf in 1976, for subtitling and sign language interpreting in the media and for specialist deaf programmes – benefiting deaf people who use sign and written language. This has focused on language and access to information, and has fundamentally changed deaf people's access to the social and leisure activities of their contemporaries through access to film, video and television. However, as already noted, the benefits of these gains for minority ethnic deaf people, who use languages other than English or versions of sign language other than BSL, are more limited. Other notable campaigns include lobbying for the 1995 Disability Discrimination Act in Britain and the Americans with Disabilities Act in the US.

The political disability movement in Britain has largely been distanced from the Deaf community's fight to be identified as a linguistic minority with their own language and culture. This may largely have resulted from the Deaf community's decision to struggle for civil rights along linguistic lines rather than on the grounds of disability (Jones and Pullen, 1989). A 1996 conference, organised by the Alliance of Deaf Service Users and Providers (ADSUP) and the Policy Studies Institute, noted in its publicity material:

> ... the lack of constructive dialogue between deaf and disabled people ... which has meant that policies and services for deaf and disabled people have tended to develop in isolation, sometimes in a climate of friction and competition for resources.

Lane (1995) discusses this conflict as a direct one between the disability and linguistic minority model. He sees late deafened and hard of hearing people as the 'core group' for the first and the Deaf community of profoundly deaf people, deaf from birth, as part of the second. Disablist notions of deafness have relied on the 'tragic' view of deafness which the medical model constructs, rather than the social construction view of deafness as a communication issue between deaf and hearing people.

The Deaf community's emphasis on language oppression leaves open the possibility that other disabled people may behave in just such a disabling manner towards deaf people as non-disabled people do towards deaf and/ or disabled people (see also, Corker 1994; Finkelstein, 1991). This has parallels for deaf people from minority ethnic communities who may experience both racist behaviour from white disabled people (Begum, 1994; Hill, 1994; Stuart, 1996; Vernon, 1996) and disablist behaviour from within their own ethnic communities. The political unease between disability and deafness movements has had an impact on the development of a separatist Deaf politics. In the same way, the unease between Deaf politics and perceived racial exclusion is encouraging the development of separate deaf facilities and politics among minority ethnic deaf people.

'Deaf politics' reflects changes that have gone on outside as well as in the Deaf community – for example, the civil rights, women's and disability rights movements are all important influences on the development of Deaf politics. Racism, sexism, disablism and homophobia have also emerged as important debates in Deaf politics.

Voluntary organisations

As discussed, the political Deaf movement has centred on language, access to information and the cultivation and sustenance of a Deaf culture and identity. Of varying importance is the part played by deaf voluntary organisations. The major national organisations are:

- The British Deaf Association (BDA), a membership organisation, mainly of Deaf people who use sign language.

- Royal National Institute for Deaf People (RNID), a large organisation involved in service provision and dealing with both deaf and hard of hearing people.

- Royal Association in Aid of Deaf People (RAD), a much smaller London-based service providing organisation.

- Hearing Concern, an organisation which represents hard of hearing people.

- National Deaf Children's Society (NDCS), an organisation which focuses on the needs of deaf children and their parents.

- National Association of Deafened People, a small group formed in 1984 around the different needs of people who become profoundly deaf as adults.

- Sense – National Deaf-blind and Rubella Association, the group for Deaf-blind people.

The United Kingdom Council on Deafness (UKCOD) is an umbrella organisation representing the above main groups and a number of other professional and language groups.

Single issue organisations also exist such as the Deaf Broadcasting Campaign, Aids Ahead (a health promotion provider), Friends of the Young Deaf and the Breakthrough Trust. There are also religious and geographically based organisations, such as the Scottish Association for the Deaf. Political lobbying has come from the larger organisations but the relatively new United Kingdom Council on Deafness is committed to bringing together the different organisations when necessary "as a single coherent voice", as Lord Ashley, Chair of the UKCOD, states in his introduction to its 1996 Annual Report.

From missions to new markets – statutory and voluntary provision

Service provision to deaf people has been divided between specialist and generic services. This has meant that the traditional specialist services centred around the social worker for deaf people usually based in a 'Centre for the Deaf', who often held responsibility for sign language interpreting. Historically, such centres were run by Christian religious organisations. The Missions for the Deaf movement, begun in the early 19th century in Scotland and well established by the middle of the century, was instrumental in setting up the College of Deaf Welfare which developed social work training courses for working with deaf people. There are mixed feelings about the achievements of missioners who, although they provided access for deaf people, themselves shared the paternalistic attitude, common to the time, towards deaf people.

Much more recently the Seebohm Report of 1968 lead to generic social work becoming the 'norm' and there was a consequent move away from specialisms in social work. This was reinforced following the 1982 Barclay Report. However, within this framework social work with deaf people remained a specialist area partly because of the interpreting role of social workers for the deaf. Through their traditionally close involvement with deaf people, social workers for the deaf are important 'gatekeepers' to the welfare state – a role often seen by deaf people as restrictive and stigmatising.

The Disabled People's Act and Community Care legislation have tended to put deaf people under the general rubric of 'disabled people'. However, the emphasis in government policy on user participation, may mean that deaf people themselves can be more involved in decision making about the delivery of services. The picture has been complicated by some voluntary organisations' increased role in service provision. The RNID, for example, funds Communication Support Agencies, which provide interpreting and other communication support.

Deaf centres have also become entrepreneurial in their attempts to keep up with the changes in the more competitive funding of services. Some, like Merseyside Centre for the Deaf, attract European funding for a range of education and training, leisure and employment provision. Deaf clubs have changed out of all recognition from the Missions for Deaf People, where they began. Deaf people are now involved at all levels of the work and often large budgets are managed to provide contracted out social work services, education and interpreting.

Ethnicity and deafness: a review

Recent years have witnessed an increasing politicisation of minority ethnic deaf people and a greater recognition of their needs on the part of services and the deaf media. This is evident in events such as the Black Deaf Conference, held in Leeds in 1991, collaboratively organised by the RNID, BDA, NDCS and two West Yorkshire local authorities. The conference brought together professionals and deaf people from minority ethnic communities in an attempt to explore ways of improving user involvement and service response. There has also been an increasing recognition of linguistic and cultural issues affecting minority ethnic deaf people in sections of the deaf media (see features in *Laserbeam,* January 1986, Spring 1987, July 1988; *See Hear,* October 1994; *British Deaf News,* April 1995; *Deafness,* July 1995). However, research evidence on ethnicity and deafness remains limited, medically oriented and largely focused on children. In particular, there is little or no research literature on the social experience of deafness, issues of language and communication, and the experiences of adults.

Minority ethnic deaf children

Much of the available research concentrates on children, particularly those of Asian origin. Studies have largely concentrated on the aetiology and epidemiology of hearing loss, especially the higher prevalence of sensori-neural hearing loss among minority ethnic groups. Naeem and Newton (1996) explored hearing loss in a comparative study of Asian and non-Asian children aged between 5 and 15 years. The hearing levels were assessed using a four frequency pure tone screening test (1kHz, 2kHz, 4kHz and 8kHz). A prevalence rate was calculated for two categories of hearing impairment (mild to profound and moderate to profound) and for the better and worse ear. The findings showed the prevalence rate for the Asian children to be higher (ranging from 5.09 to 9.61 per 1,000) than the non-Asian children (1.4 to 3.51 per 1,000). Asian children had 2.42 to 3.61 times greater risk of having a hearing loss than non-Asian children. This confirms the findings of an earlier study conducted in Bradford which found that the prevalence of hearing loss was 3.5 times greater for the Asian children compared to the non-Asian children (Lumb, 1981), although less marked differences are reported by Cooper (1995). The 'Asian' sample in these studies largely consisted of Pakistani children.

Considerably greater prevalence is reported in recent work on

Bangladeshi children by Vanniasegaram et al (1993). They report the prevalence of hearing loss of 50 dB or greater to be over six times the national average among the Bangladeshi population living in Tower Hamlets. Mendelian deafness was identified as the most common form of sensori-neural hearing loss affecting the Bangladeshi children in this sample and was thought to have occurred as a consequence of consanguineous marriage patterns. Chamba et al (1998) report that many practitioners and parents considered consanguinity as an explanatory factor for the raised prevalence of deafness in Asian children; Ahmad (1994) provides a critique of the consanguinity discourse. Ongoing research on genetics and deafness in relation to Asian children includes the work led by Professor Bob Mueller at St James' and Seacroft University Hospital Trust in Leeds and Dr Adrian Davis at the Institute of Hearing Research in Nottingham.

A limited amount of work has been published relating to issues of communication, patterns of language use and speech acquisition among minority ethnic families with a deaf child. Bangladeshi deaf children have been the subject of most studies which have been undertaken in this area (Bellman and Marcuson, 1991; Mahon et al, 1995). Mahon et al's work highlights some of the difficulties experienced by families bringing up a deaf child in a multilingual environment. Through an investigation of conversational strategies employed in Bangladeshi families, their work shows how mothers' ability to communicate effectively with their deaf children was severely hampered by their own lack of knowledge of English and the children's lack of understanding of Sylheti, their mother tongue. In such circumstances, misunderstandings commonly occurred between mother and child which were rarely resolved and ultimately lead to breakdowns in communication. Mahon et al concluded that professionals need to understand more about language use among families whose first language is not English, claiming that this would improve the way in which deaf children from non-English speaking families were treated by professionals, particularly in the early stages of their education and rehabilitation. Issues of communication and education are also addressed by Chamba et al (in press).

A growing number of studies have emerged out of a concern about the ability of mainstream service providers to meet the needs of deaf people from minority ethnic communities. Bellman and Marcuson (1991) looked at the problems faced in assessing the hearing of deaf children with greater fluency in their mother tongue than in English or sign language. Problems are caused by audiology professionals not having sufficient skills in the child's first language to assess the degree of language development. In recognition of this fact and using the districts of Tower Hamlets, Hackney and Islington as a focus for their work, the authors developed a relatively inexpensive and easily administered test known as the EL2 Toy Set. Chamba et al (1998) discuss the potential problems of distraction testing for hearing in children whose home language is not English, citing the mispronunciation of Asian names by English-speaking professionals as an example.

Lynas and Turner (1995) examined the extent to which educational services for pre-school hearing impaired children were meeting the needs of minority ethnic children. They were struck by the gross variation in the distribution of minority ethnic deaf children in different parts of the country. In some areas, minority ethnic deaf children formed the majority user-group of educational services while in other areas they were non-existent. They noted that although considerable efforts were being made towards sensitive and effective service delivery by some local education authorities, there was generally a need for more staff training in cultural awareness issues and the employment of staff with appropriate skills in languages used by families.

Chamba et al (1998) shed light on parent–practitioner interaction around the diagnosis of deafness in pre-school Asian children. Parents confronted delays in diagnosis and often coped with limited information about the condition or support services. Communication problems exacerbated problems of access and parents resented the poor organisation of services and dismissive attitude of some staff. Examples of this were the unreliable appointments system and the opaqueness of why different children from the same family were often seen in two separate provider units. Support around diagnosis and disclosure of deafness was regarded as poor by many parents and they were often confused about the roles of different professionals from various agencies. However, parents highly valued the advice and support provided by the peripatetic teachers of the deaf, who often acted as the parents' key contact with services.

Currently, the NDCS is engaged in a review of its services to minority ethnic deaf children. The related publications will be a useful addition to the limited literature on social aspects of deafness and provision of support to parents (Melissa James, personal communication). However, as Gregory et al (1995) note, research on minority ethnic children's and young people's own experiences remains limited.

Minority ethnic deaf adults

Relatively little is written on the experience of minority ethnic deaf adults, part of the 'other deaf community' as it is called in the Open University's excellent *Issues in Deafness* course (1991 and 1995).

The only major studies on deaf adults have been conducted by the two major deaf voluntary organisations, RNID (Badat and Whall-Roberts, 1994) and RAD (Sharma and Love, 1991). The aim of both studies was to identify issues and obstacles facing minority ethnic deaf people. In both cases, interviews were conducted with a wide range of service providers as well as with minority ethnic deaf people. The findings of the RNID study were based on the views of Asian deaf people living in the West Yorkshire region and Asian, African Caribbean and African deaf people in London. Deaf people in both areas knew little about the services to which they were entitled, such as benefits and hearing aids, and found it difficult to access information and thus missed out on services. Similarly, many had limited awareness of their own culture, religion and community customs as a result of being educated in a 'white' environment and not having access to their home language. The RAD report also identified a range of needs which were not being met by mainstream services in areas such as education, employment and social services.

Not surprisingly, these studies highlighted major gaps in health and social care provision and made recommendations for improved service delivery. They were important for providing insights into everyday problems encountered by minority ethnic deaf people and stressed the need for greater sensitivity and awareness on the part of employers and service-providing organisations. Recommendations to organisations included recruitment, training and improved career prospects for minority ethnic staff, especially deaf people. It was also felt that there was a need to set up mechanisms within organisations to enable minority ethnic deaf people to influence decision making and be involved in service planning. Just as importantly, the researchers felt that there was a need to gain a more accurate picture of the numbers of deaf and hard of hearing people from minority ethnic communities at both local levels and nationally. They also emphasised the need to involve hearing people in promoting deaf awareness among different minority ethnic communities.

These findings were substantiated by a smaller-scale study among Asian deaf and hard of hearing adults in Leicester of user views about social service provision (Kohli, 1990). This study also identified counselling as a much needed service for Asian deaf people as well as for their families.

On the whole, existing research on minority ethnic deaf people remains limited and does not reflect the wider increased interest in deafness as an area of scholarly and research activity. Further, there is no research study which focuses on developments in ethnicity and deafness at a broad level.

Conclusion

Deaf people are not all the same. They use different sign and spoken languages and contain the diversity observed in hearing people. The culture, languages and politics of deafness have changed dramatically over the last 40 years, partly as the result of the recognition of sign language and the consequent organisation around the idea of deaf people as a linguistic minority. The emergence of the political deaf movement has led to an uneasy relationship with the political disability movement as many Deaf people, identifying themselves as part of the Deaf community and using sign language, do not see themselves as disabled. These changes in Deaf politics have implications for all deaf people although many may not wish to be identified with the Deaf world (Lane et al, 1996). The impact which these changes have had on policy and services through user involvement has meant that a more assertive role is required from the hard of hearing and deafened and deaf-blind people in making clear their own distinct needs in order to gain access to resources.

Service delivery to deaf people has been dominated by the language debate between sign and spoken language and disablist notions about the innate tragedy of deafness. The reaction to the 'audist' establishments of health and education services (although views and practices are not homogenous), in particular, has helped to create a strong Deaf community based on sign language. Equally, deaf people are now acknowledging their own diversity in terms of ethnicity, language, culture and sexuality. Deaf people from minority ethnic communities are creating their own structures and networks within both the Deaf and hearing worlds, an issue which comes out strongly in the chapters to follow.

Chapter 4 provides a national overview of a range of initiatives involving minority ethnic deaf people.

Minority ethnic deaf people: a national overview of initiatives and services

A number of relatively consistent themes emerge in the literature on welfare services and minority ethnic communities which provide a useful background to this discussion of minority ethnic deaf people and service initiatives. More detailed discussion of some of these issues is available in Ahmad (1993), Ahmad and Atkin (1996b), Butt and Mirza (1996), Jeyasingham (1992) and McNaught (1987) and see also Chapter 2.

First, the culture of 'specialist' services, so beloved of service providers, is alive and important to consider. Common to specialist provision in a range of fields are characteristics such as ad-hocism, short-termism, unpredictability regarding future funding, and the tendency for the work to expand beyond the original remit. Second, the focus of many initiatives is on issues around language, communication and information where responses are often reduced to translated materials, interpreters or, occasionally, bilingual workers. Third, developments in the voluntary sector have often reflected fashions in identity politics and official concerns about identity conflict, especially about the supposed identity vacuum facing the second and third generation of minority ethnic young people. Age, gender and ethnicity are potentially important factors here and may in themselves provide strong organising axes. An interesting phenomenon of the 1980s' adherence to the notion of a political 'black' identity was that, while this offered a potent organising and campaigning symbol at a national level or in struggles with officialdom, few grass-roots initiatives were organised at such broad levels. Often, linguistic and cultural needs or demographic patterns made it practical sense to organise within ethnic and religious boundaries, and within this often by gender. Such identity politics may be reflected in the organisation of deaf services.

A fourth factor in specialist provision is what we may call the 'specialist worker' phenomenon. Waseem Aladdin, an Asian psychologist, refers to this as the 'this one is for you' phenomenon: the assumption that once a 'specialist worker' is in place all minority ethnic cases will necessarily pass on to this worker (Alladin, 1992). Other white workers use this to 'disqualify' themselves from responsibilities to service all sections of the community. The net effect may indeed be the provision of an unequal service to minority ethnic users, by someone in a marginal position in a predominantly white-dominated organisation. Such workers also commonly experience hostility from white colleagues and are isolated.

Finally, developments in services have traditionally been multiply skewed; most initiatives cover specific issues (for example, health conditions) or specific minorities, and are located in mainly urban areas of high minority ethnic concentration. Many small minority ethnic communities as well as the numerically large but dispersed groups (for example, Chinese) remain forgotten. Many of these concerns are apparent in the limited literature on ethnicity and deafness (Sharma and Love, 1991; Badat and Whall-Roberts, 1994). These themes are important in considering the development of initiatives and services involving or aimed at deaf people from minority ethnic communities.

Here we provide a national overview of provision involving minority ethnic deaf people, based on information collected from a postal and telephone survey (details of the methods used are given in the Appendix). We begin by considering developments in or supported by social and educational services before focusing on social and cultural activity. We then examine developments in hearing and speech and language therapy. Service initiatives aimed at older deaf people and deaf people with mental health problems are briefly considered and the final two sections focus on initiatives concerning information and resources survey. Details of the specific projects mentioned are available in Darr et al (1997).

Developments in social and community services

Significant developments in service provision have taken place in areas of relatively large minority ethnic concentration, such as West Yorkshire, Lancashire, the Midlands and parts of London. A number of projects have also been identified in Wales and Northern Ireland.

Some social services departments, particularly in London, reported communication problems with non-English speaking deaf people. Service users ranged from deaf members of settled minority communities to those belonging to refugee groups from Somalia, former Yugoslavia and Ethiopia. Communication was particularly difficult when users had no knowledge of BSL or of English and community language interpreters were frequently called upon to help out. Ideally it would make sense to use a sign language interpreter with community language skills in these circumstances, but there is a shortage of sign language interpreters from minority ethnic communities. Many Deaf people have expressed their desire for sign language interpreters who understand their ethnic identity and are familiar with culturally appropriate signs, terms and names.

As part of their efforts to make services more accessible, a few social services departments had appointed minority ethnic staff. However, only five minority ethnic social workers with deaf people were identified – all Asian hearing females with the exception of one who was hard of hearing. None had been employed to work specifically with deaf people from their own communities although their caseloads were more likely to consist of Asian deaf people. This largely resulted from the perception of other workers that they were unable to offer an appropriate service to Asian clients.

These social workers felt that it was important to network with each other, partly because there were so few of them working with Asian deaf people but also because some felt isolated working in a white environment, often with unsympathetic colleagues. As a result of working closely with Asian deaf people and knowing the social problems and pressures their clients faced, these workers had developed aspects of their work to cater better for the personal, cultural and religious needs of users. An important aspect of their work was counselling, especially for deaf adolescents whom they perceived to be in a state of identity confusion and needing help in making decisions about their future, often without any assistance from hearing family members. Consideration of choice of marriage partners caused distress among Asian deaf youth and their parents.

Asian social workers were also aware that their service needed to be responsive to the needs and concerns of parents of Asian deaf children. They identified appropriate religious education of the children, thought to be central to their socialisation and development of cultural identity, as a major parental concern. Social workers frequently supported parents frustrated at their own inability to explain aspects of their religion and culture to their children. Social workers were equally concerned that the religious needs of Asian children were being overlooked by service providers and were making attempts to resolve this problem. Examples include help in finding a suitable tutor to teach young deaf children to read the Quran and setting up a support group for mothers of Asian deaf children. Such support was particularly lacking for other minority ethnic groups.

Developments in educational services

A small number of education authorities had established services to support deaf children whose mother language was not English. Our research identified initiatives with deaf children and their families in Bradford, Kirklees, Leeds, Derby, Tower Hamlets, Coventry and Rochdale. These focused on the educational, social and communication needs of minority ethnic deaf children and emphasised parental involvement in children's education. Parents were given accessible information and workers also carried out home visits and accompanied parents to hospital and clinics when necessary.

Other education authorities had not appointed specialist workers but had made modifications to their service delivery to ensure they met the language needs of minority ethnic deaf children and their families. In many cases this meant bilingual workers or interpreters working closely with staff employed to provide services for deaf children. Most commonly, workers assisted deaf children in mainstream schools, liaised between the home and school and interpreted information for reviews and consultations with parents. The areas with such provision included Stratford, Shrewsbury, Stockport, Manchester and, in Scotland, Falkirk.

Efforts were also being made to bridge the communication gap between deaf children from non-English speaking backgrounds and their hearing parents. The most obvious way in which this was being achieved was by encouraging parents to learn sign language and participate more in the child's education and school life. We identified nine sign language classes established for parents whose first language was not English, largely used by Asian parents. The majority were organised by local education authorities, although a social services department was responsible for one such service. Some of these classes also functioned as support groups where parents were encouraged to share experiences and concerns.

Although these classes were not targeted specifically at mothers, the majority of users were women. Classes were weekly, in the daytime, and usually provided free transport. The method by which sign language or sign-supported English was taught varied: some were run by white tutors, usually hearing, while others used an Asian language interpreter to work alongside a sign language tutor. This differs from most BSL teaching which tends to be carried out by BSL first language users who are deaf themselves. The classes were not aimed to lead to BSL qualification; rather the aim was simply to enable parents to enhance their signing skills and help improve communication with their deaf child.

Several initiatives were identified around adult learning, some of which targeted specific groups such as Somalis in Cardiff, Asians in Leicester or refugees in London. Most of these recognised the difficulties facing deaf youth in securing employment and took a multiagency approach to providing appropriate training. The Cardiff project was aimed at Somali deaf people who had little or no English language skills and involved a social worker in conjunction with a Somali community worker and a local college. An English as a Second Language (ESL) tutor worked closely with a BSL interpreter to improve the students' communication skills. The project had helped only a few Somalis so far but funding was expected to continue this work. The project based in Leicester was a joint initiative between the local council, the Centre for Deaf People and the Adult Education Centre. Work preparation courses were organised by a tutor from a minority ethnic community, followed by sessions provided by an adult guidance worker offering educational and careers advice with the help of a BSL interpreter. Unfortunately the project only lasted for one year as it was regarded as too expensive to fund such highly individualised training.

City Lit Centre for Deaf People at the City Lit College for Adult Education in London had developed adult education courses for deaf people from minority ethnic communities. This included 'New Start' courses for newly arrived deaf people which covered language and communication skills, literacy and numeracy as well as an introduction to 'British culture'.

Deaf social and cultural groups

The most noticeable way in which minority ethnic deaf people have organised themselves is through forming social and cultural groups. A number of such groups were identified, the majority organised by Asian deaf people and found in Bradford, Leicester, Coventry, Manchester, Birmingham and London. Although these groups were open to all Asian people irrespective of nationality or religion, in some parts of the country they had understandably attracted members of the largest Asian communities settled in that area. Hence in Bradford, one deaf cultural group, although notionally open to all Asian deaf youth was, in practice, attended only by Pakistani Muslim deaf youth. Similarly in Leicester, a social group for hard of hearing Asian people was made up exclusively of Indian Gujaratis. On the other hand, some larger groups, such as the Asian Deaf Women's Association based in London and the Coventry Deaf Asian youth group, consisted of deaf individuals from a range of ethnic backgrounds. These groups combined social and cultural activities with information sharing and learning. Many of the nationally organised social events were aimed at deaf people from different minority ethnic communities.

African Caribbean clubs were largely based in London, apart from one in the Midlands. The London clubs were organised along the lines of Deaf clubs generally: they were run by a committee made up of members and had a social club atmosphere based around food, social activities and sport with some emphasis on education and networking with other clubs. The clubs had a strong emphasis on deaf children and young people.

Some of these groups catered for a particular target group, such as youth or women, while others had a broader membership. Only one group was identified which catered for the needs of hard of hearing people and similarly only one for the families of Asian deaf young people. Generally speaking, African Caribbean and Asian social groups tended to organise as mutually exclusive groups; there were very few examples where they came together. Exceptions to this included a group running from a residential centre for deaf people with learning difficulties as well as two voluntary groups, in Cleveland and Brixton. Organisers of these latter groups had found no reason to create ethnically segregated groups, partly due to the fact that they were catering for small numbers and partly because members were happy with an ethnically mixed environment.

Setting up social groups

Social groups were set up either by service providers working with deaf people or by deaf people themselves. In either case, it was recognised that some kind of separate social provision was needed because mainstream services were not catering to the needs of minority ethnic deaf people. Furthermore, among service providers there was a growing recognition of isolation, confusion and powerlessness among the minority ethnic deaf people, particularly young people. It was felt that in setting up social groups, these problems could be addressed by bringing people together to discuss and share their experiences. Regular meetings, on a weekly or monthly basis, meant that members could create links and develop friendships in supportive surroundings.

Social groups acquired funding from a number of sources and with varying degrees of difficulty. If the impetus for setting up a group came from social services, funding was likely to come from their department. Only four of the social groups were funded in this way. Others had acquired funding from other sources, such as health and local authorities, particularly youth and leisure departments or businesses and fundraising.

Although their primary aim was almost always social, as the groups developed they set out their own agendas in response to the needs of their members. All used these sessions to discuss a range of issues: commonly, concerns about religion, culture and ethnic identity. Youth groups in particular were keen to learn more about customs, traditions and festivals which seemed to form an important part of their families' lives and from which they felt excluded. Indeed a number of Asian deaf groups were organising parties to celebrate religious festivals such as Eid and Diwali and these occasions were used to network with similar groups in other parts of the country.

Alongside these mixed purpose groups, the 'party movement' was increasing in strength and popularity. The minority ethnic Deaf parties began in the early 1990s and have brought together people from throughout the UK. The parties are centred around food and socialising and are often organised to celebrate festivals. Although formally open to all deaf people, these parties tend to have largely Asian and African Caribbean participants. One local group organiser noted the lack of involvement of white deaf people:

> "They [white deaf people] complain that we shut them out, but they don't come. It's not that we shut them out."

Being part of a social group with people of a similar background meant that deaf people could discuss sensitive issues such as marriage and family life. It also allowed them to voice concerns over the way in which they were treated as deaf people within their own communities.

Training courses were considered to be important by most groups. These ranged from educational courses in BSL and basic English to those promoting assertiveness, confidence-building and youth-work training. One group had organised an arts and crafts workshop while another regularly held sessions on cookery, haircare and beauty.

All of the groups saw one of their roles as providing advice and information on benefits and services. Many deaf people and families with deaf children were unclear about their entitlements. Some organisers regularly invited speakers from various agencies to talk about services with the aid of a sign language interpreter.

A number of initiatives had been set up specifically to promote religious awareness among deaf people from minority ethnic communities. The Catholic Deaf Association (often based around Irish communities) has been running as a national organisation for more than 30 years. Over this period it has facilitated deaf people's attendance at church services and promoted interaction between deaf and hearing Catholics. It currently organises a variety of activities and training courses so that Catholic deaf people are better informed about their faith and has made efforts to ensure that their churches are better designed to cater for the needs of their deaf and hard of hearing members. Similarly, the professional Missions for the Deaf movement has a long history of association with 'Deaf welfare' and the establishment of Deaf churches and Deaf clubs. There are still chaplains for deaf people working for the Church of England Deaf Society.

Very few initiatives existed for minority ethnic groups other than Asians and African Caribbeans. We identified two Jewish organisations in London – Koleinu and the Jewish Deaf Association – which were active in promoting the Jewish faith as well as providing general support to deaf people. Aspects of Jewish religion and culture were also explored in a workshop which was organised by the Nuffield Hearing and Speech Centre in London and attended by Jewish youth and adults. A similar workshop was also held for hearing and deaf Greek parents which examined the educational and language choices for their deaf children. Our research has not identified any initiatives working with other small or dispersed minority ethnic groups such as Chinese deaf people.

At a broader level, the growing number of minority ethnic disability organisations have also managed to recruit deaf people as members. Such initiatives have been set up in Bradford, Walsall, Birmingham, Coventry and various parts of London. Their aims are to inform and advise minority ethnic disabled people about disability issues and to make service providers aware of their needs. In Hackney, the Disability Equality Unit has employed a hard of hearing Asian Information Outreach Worker who runs a weekly surgery to enable Asian disabled people to obtain council services. Two other projects focusing on childhood disability operate in Cardiff and Reading and include deafness within their remit. Their focus is on informing, educating and empowering parents about services and enabling them to make informed decisions about their children's future.

Initiatives in the health service

There has been a growing concern about the lack of appropriate methods to measure language development of deaf children for whom a decision has been made to pursue oral education and who are exposed to a number of different spoken languages in the home environment. Standard tests for measuring spoken language used by speech and language therapy departments and audiology clinics are carried out in English which disadvantages children who communicate in other languages. Over recent years, steps have been taken by a small number of speech and language therapy departments to make their services appropriate to all sections of their users.

For example, speech and language therapy departments in Walsall, Leicester and Nottingham have all taken steps to develop work in this area. All three are concerned with the low take-up of services by minority ethnic people, though not just deaf people. The possibilities for positive change are exemplified by the developments in Leicester, where the Fosse Health Trust has appointed a specialist speech and language therapist and two bilingual co-workers to improve the service to its non-English speaking clients. The Asian speech and language therapist has had the responsibility of coordinating this aspect of the service and has promoted her role so that other speech and language therapists are able to refer clients to her for assessment. The co-workers, who have skills in Punjabi, Gujarati and Urdu, have developed action plans to work on specific aims to further their role in the department. These range from assisting therapists with assessments of new clients to learning more about the theoretical and clinical aspects of their work. It is hoped that the co-workers and the specialist speech therapist will inform and educate professionals such as general practitioners and health visitors about culturally appropriate and sensitive service delivery, including more appropriate testing. Alongside these improvements, the department has expanded its stock of multicultural resources by translating information into the main Asian community languages. The co-workers have been engaged in outreach work to inform communities about the role of the speech and language therapy department. In order to evaluate service delivery, consumer quality questionnaires have been devised for new deaf users and parents of deaf children.

Walsall and Nottingham were developing their speech and language therapy services along similar lines. In Walsall, the speech and language therapy department was examining its assessment procedure to address the low take-up of services among people from ethnic minorities. Such developments are promising for parents who choose to educate their children orally and reflect the fact that service providers are making an effort to improve their services.

Services for older deaf people

Little is known about the extent of acquired deafness among older members of ethnic minority groups. Older hard of hearing or deafened people are often unaware that advice and support is available, especially when they do not use English well. Efforts were being made by staff in social services departments in areas such as Bradford and Newham to alert older people to the environmental aids and entitlements for people losing their hearing later in life. In Leicester, a social group at the Deaf centre catered for the needs of mainly older, hard of hearing Asian people, and was greatly valued by all its members.

Two projects were identified, in Bradford and Sheffield, which had worked in the area of industrial deafness among older people. Both were funded by Occupational Health Units in the early 1990s and aimed to uncover the extent of occupational deafness among former mill and factory workers. Those identified as deaf due to industrial noise were supported to claim compensation. The work in Sheffield targeted the Yemeni, African Caribbean and Pakistani communities while in Bradford the focus was on Pakistani and Bangladeshi communities, with both projects conducting hearing tests in accessible venues such as community centres. The success of these projects in contacting large number of people points to an area of unmet need.

Our research found diverse approaches to ethnic sensitivity in service provision. For example, two audiology departments, Edinburgh and Cleveland, were offering hearing aids and moulds in shades to match the users' skin colour, the traditional pink aids and moulds regarded by both users and professionals as inappropriate for many of their service users. We have already noted sign language teaching for Asian parents and, in some schools, attempts to provide information on minority cultures and religions.

Deafness and mental health

The mental health of deaf people is becoming an increasingly important issue, illustrated by the emergence of national and European organisations for deafness and mental health. We found only limited efforts being made by services to address this problem in relation to minority ethnic deaf people. The National Centre for Mental Health and Deafness, based in Manchester, stands out from mainstream services as an organisation committed to ensuring that patients' needs are catered for, regardless of their ethnic background. The Centre employs a consultant psychiatrist, himself from a minority ethnic background, who is keen to promote deaf awareness among the Asian community. He has been responsible for appointing an Asian counsellor to the Centre and changing aspects of service delivery to make it more culturally sensitive. The Centre is now equipped with a prayer room, used by deaf adults and parents of deaf children, and it takes the dietary habits of its users into consideration when devising menus.

Information and resources

There is a shortage of information available in languages other than English about deafness, although efforts are being made, mainly by health trusts and voluntary organisations, to improve this situation. Audiology departments in Harrow and Burton have produced information about hearing tests in South Asian languages and the Paediatric Cochlear Implant Programme has produced a variety of materials in these languages as well as in Welsh. Information about tinnitus has been made available in Asian languages by the RNID and the British Tinnitus Association.

The NDCS has perhaps made the greatest progress in making its information more accessible to members of ethnic minorities. Translated information is available in South Asian languages and in Welsh on a variety of topics including education, hearing aids, glue ear, speech and language therapy and Disability Living Allowance. A Welsh language information leaflet has also been produced by Ceredigion Community Health Council about aids to communication for deaf people.

Videos have been seen as another useful way of disseminating information about deafness to parents of deaf children who cannot speak English. Two short videos have been produced by Tower Hamlets Health Promotion Service which are targeted at primary healthcare professionals and parents of Bengali deaf children. They aim to alert mothers of deaf children to the early signs of deafness and help them come to terms with having a deaf child. Another video for parents of deaf children has been produced by the ABCD project based in Cardiff, in conjunction with the NDCS. This addresses the nature of deafness as well as the diagnosis and assessment procedure and has been subtitled into the main Asian community languages.

Another useful video targeted at Asian parents of young deaf children has been produced by Bradford Education Authority. It is a sign language video of common phrases which a parent would use to communicate with a deaf child. Each phrase shown in sign language is accompanied by a voice over in an Asian language explaining the meaning of the phrase. The video is felt to be a useful resource by parents who use it for reference within their own homes and also as a way of teaching members of the wider family how to communicate at a basic level with the deaf child.

Conclusion

The encouraging message from this overview of initiatives is that many agencies and organisations are beginning to address the needs of minority ethnic deaf people. At the same time, minority ethnic deaf people and their families are organising to provide for a range of needs, particularly around cultural and religious values. In other ways there are strong parallels between developments in services for minority ethnic deaf people and those for minority ethnic people generally. This chapter offers a rapid snapshot of developments in these areas, as already stated, but fuller details of individual projects can be found in Darr et al (1997). Many of these issues are explored in depth in the chapters to follow while Chapter 9 locates the findings in wider literature.

Chapter 5 explores initiatives around ethnicity and identity in relation to minority ethnic deaf people.

"I send my child to school and he comes back an Englishman": identity politics, self-help and services

Identity construction and maintenance through organised activity is an important aspect of the lives of minority ethnic deaf people (see Chapter 2). Among the variety of initiatives on ethnicity and disability identified in Chapter 4, those which are user-led largely concentrate on social, cultural and religious issues and can be seen in terms of a quest for rediscovering and cultivating identities other than those defined by deafness. Here we discuss these initiatives in depth and explore issues of identity politics and its links with a range of self-help based, voluntary and statutory sector initiatives.

A number of important issues in relation to the construction and negotiation of identities in the lives of minority ethnic deaf people are explored in this chapter. First, the importance of religion and culture from the perspectives of young people, their parents and workers is addressed, including the attempts which are made to impart religious and cultural values to deaf children. Second, the emergence of social and cultural groups is explored in terms of their focus, organisation and value to users. These groups raise interesting questions about multiple identities (deafness, gender, religion, ethnicity) and their negotiation. The diversity of responses to identity politics parallels that found in the wider literature on ethnicity and identity (Drury, 1991; Modood et al, 1994). Third, the importance of learning and networking through various initiatives is traced, addressing how this empowers and informs people, facilitates supportive networks and enables improved communication between families and their deaf members. Fourth, we focus on some developments in mainstream services aimed at making them more ethnically sensitive although, as we will see, this does not constitute a marked cultural shift. Finally, we discuss various respondents' perspectives on the need for 'specialist' provision, although we use this term loosely; counselling and sign language interpreting are discussed in particular.

This and subsequent chapters are based on an analysis of in-depth interviews with minority ethnic deaf people and workers with deaf people (see the Appendix for details of methods).

Religion and culture

Parents we talked to found it particularly difficult to convey aspects of their cultural and religious background to their children and many were concerned that the children knew more about the 'British' way of life than the cultural values and traditions of their parents and ethnic community. A Bengali bilingual worker who had close contact with Bengali deaf children talked about the tensions faced by the parents she visited:

> "They find it [culture and religion] extremely difficult to explain and they live in a Western society. Whereas they want to hold onto their traditions and things but they can't because they can't explain things to them and if they argue too much they end up fighting and then the kids will want to go and leave home and things."

Even when deaf children had acquired a basic understanding of their religion from their parents, all too often they were not provided with adequate explanations for these religious beliefs. This was simply because many parents and children shared no common language in which to communicate complex concepts. As a result of limited access to information, many deaf children grew up with rigid ideas about their religion with little understanding of scope for negotiation of religious observance. This limited understanding compromised the deaf person's ability to regard and use religion or culture as a flexible resource providing broad guidelines within which behaviour can be negotiated (Ahmad, 1996).

An Asian sign language interpreter explained her view of how ideas about religion were internalised by the deaf person:

> "... if you look at hearing Asian people, yeah, you hear something and then you think, ignore it, because you know it's nonsense, you know, you must tie your hair up because, whatever and you know it's ... your choice. Well with deaf people, because they don't have, um ... access to that wider

> debate, if you see what I mean, if you tell them something,
> that is it and they have to do it that way...."

An Asian Deaf outreach worker extended this problem to lack of knowledge about other areas of life, such as marriage functions:

> "I've met lots of Asian deaf people who don't understand
> what a dowry is.... They don't understand that issue at all.
> They don't know the language so they don't understand what
> it means that way ... they don't understand why the wedding
> is large. They don't understand anything about the marriage
> ceremonies or anything, the dowries, they don't even
> understand that, it's a very basic thing. I think it's a
> problem...."

Lack of a common language often leads to the exclusion of deaf people from family and community events. A Jewish Deaf young man who, having grown up as part of the Jewish hearing community, recalled occasions on which deaf people were excluded from joining in ceremonies such as Bar Mitzvah.

This gap in cultural knowledge was not filled by the education service. Many respondents felt that schools were doing little to provide information about minority religions and cultures, although some were making attempts to provide such information. One school for deaf children had invited a hearing voluntary worker to address school assemblies on Islam. This Pakistani man had good signing skills and a strong commitment to promoting greater religious awareness among the younger deaf people. He felt that the limited religious and cultural awareness among Asian deaf children was an important issue for both deaf young people and their families. Few accessible resources were able to facilitate such learning and he was critical of the role of services:

> "... whether it's from social services or from the health
> authority, none of them's providing it and education's not
> providing it either."

This view was reiterated by a Bengali mother who was concerned at her son's lack of awareness of his own culture, her concerns summed up in the comment:

> "I send my child to school and he comes back an Englishman."

To combat these problems, many parents of deaf children and deaf people themselves were engaged in a variety of activities. Responses from parents included obtaining information in Asian languages from Pakistan or India and lobbying deaf organisations to cater for the cultural and religious needs of children and their families.

It was usually only after finishing compulsory schooling that many deaf young people realised their relative lack of knowledge about their own ethnicity, history and culture. This limited knowledge was a cause of regret and resentment to many but the process of rediscovering and reclaiming cultural and religious identities was felt to be empowering. For example, one deaf woman of Indian origin, was reaffirming her cultural identity by rediscovering Indian clothing, foods and adornments. This process of rediscovery both reflected empowerment and was itself empowering.

> **"I never really considered myself as an Asian person. I was very ashamed to wear bangles and I was very ashamed to wear saris.... I think in the past, I fooled myself in the past. Really I think it has taken me 15 years to reach where I am today. Now I feel much more positive."**

However, not having been taught any Hindi as a child, she felt excluded from aspects of Indian culture and history – a dilemma faced by many deaf people from minority ethnic groups.

The problem was regarded as even greater for some other groups. For example, an African Caribbean Deaf youth worker highlighted the need for better access to information relevant to the lives of African Caribbean Deaf young people:

> **"Black and Asian hearing people have their own magazines which incorporates their culture and history, everything, it's beautiful. There is nothing historical for black, deaf people."**

Although there is considerable academic and popular literature on Africa and African Caribbean people, this was regarded as inaccessible for Deaf people. Further, the perceived lack of African Caribbean Deaf role models was felt to make it harder for African Caribbean Deaf young people to develop and sustain a positive ethnic identity.

Having gained only a limited understanding of their own ethnic identity, it is not surprising that many deaf children from minority ethnic communities had grown up with confused notions of their ethnic and religious identity and relationships with the wider society. For many, it appeared only natural that they should see themselves first and foremost as 'Deaf people', belonging to the 'Deaf community', albeit a predominantly white deaf community. The possible stronger affiliation with Deaf people was often related to language as a means to and signifier of alliances. Some members of an Asian Deaf youth group we interviewed felt that sharing a common language (that is, BSL) made it easier for minority ethnic Deaf people to identify with other Deaf people rather than with members of their own community:

> "Asian [Deaf] women was more closer to Deaf community than to anybody else because they're Deaf first and then Asian.... I think Deaf, it's all different really, Deaf community is Deaf first then Asian because even for the Asian Deaf their way of communication is via BSL, [or] in English, so they're more happy to use their skills with a Deaf person rather than an Asian family who doesn't communicate...."

That some Deaf people's families or ethnic communities made little attempt to learn BSL or about deaf issues, partly explained and justified the stronger affiliation of some Deaf people with Deaf white people compared to hearing people of their own ethnic background. For many Deaf people, whichever minority ethnic community they belonged to, identity affiliations were not easy, as one white social services manager pointed out:

> "A lot of people have trouble accepting that Deaf people have their own community, culture, etceteras, but what happens if you're black or you're Asian and Deaf as well ... which are you first? You know, are you Asian first and then Deaf or are you Deaf and then Asian, or whatever. And to actually have to deal with two lots of different culture and also have white hearing culture as well in everyday surroundings ... even Deaf people themselves don't take that on board."

There were variations in the level of awareness about religion and community culture among different minority ethnic groups. The Irish Deaf groups within the United Kingdom had a strong Catholic emphasis and the Northern Irish and Scottish Deaf Associations were sometimes based around religious groups. Historically, the Church Mission Society provided many of the first Deaf clubs and still trains chaplains for the Deaf and funds Deaf churches. Members of the Jewish Deaf community were also thought to have acquired a high level of religious awareness through involvement with established Jewish Deaf organisations. In contrast, Asian and African Caribbean Deaf people were still in the process of discovering their respective religious and cultural identities, largely through self-organisation. In particular, many felt that young African Caribbean Deaf people have very little relevant provision in this area. There appeared to be little evidence of Deaf people from minority ethnic communities becoming religious leaders as in the Church of England where a Deaf woman priest had been ordained.

Emergence of social and cultural groups

Since the early 1990s there has been a growing recognition among service providers as well as minority ethnic deaf individuals that mainstream services to deaf people do not take account of cultural and religious needs. There has also been an increased awareness of racist attitudes and practices in the white Deaf community and mainstream services which marginalise deaf people from minority ethnic communities. Partly as a consequence, but equally as examples of self-help organised around important aspects of ethnic or religious life, a number of social groups have emerged in various parts of the country which aim to address social, cultural and information needs.

We found that these groups varied considerably in terms of membership, funding sources, accountability and level of user involvement. Some consisted of Deaf people who had united on the basis of their 'blackness', while others targeted Deaf people who belonged to a specific ethnic group or had a particular religious affiliation. There were also groups which were exclusively for Asian Deaf women. One group of this nature came into existence as a result of an Asian Deaf woman recognising that there was no social provision for women like herself. By contacting the youth service and securing funding from the local community education service she was able to set up this group. In its five-year lifespan, the group had attracted a membership of around 100 Asian deaf women and is now run by an information and outreach worker with the help of a volunteer, both Asian Deaf women. Not only did they provide information on religious and cultural issues and celebrate festivals, such as Diwali, Eid and Christmas, they also provided health and welfare advice both on an individual basis and through inviting speakers from outside agencies. Women's health was the focus of another African Caribbean Deaf group which also ran sessions on topics such as sexual and women's health and relationships.

Most such groups combined social activities with welfare advice, although the range of available activities depended very much on the resources and the needs identified by members. Younger members of these groups particularly enjoyed the social and sporting activities and were eager for more outdoor activities. A hard of hearing group of older Gujarati people valued the information they were provided about environmental aids and adaptations as well as the opportunity to talk about problems with their hearing aids, text telephones and other issues. Members, many of them not fluent in English, found it helpful to have information in Gujarati from the Gujarati community development worker. However one profoundly deafened member of the group complained that his communication needs were being overlooked by the group organisers and lack of resources. Although an English volunteer was available to write down for him what was happening within the group sessions, this was problematic as the worker had no knowledge of Gujarati, unlike the previous volunteer. Ideally this elderly man needed a Gujarati-language note-taker to provide a written commentary of the proceedings. He expressed his isolation in writing:

> **"... this group hasn't much trouble with hearing ... they have always loop on their ear. The trouble with this group is that they can't probably understand, speak, write English language, hence they need [Gujarati] interpreter ... it is actually people like me who are profound deaf needs help to remain in contact through writing. There is nothing for me [here] now."**

The final comment referred to the fact that the group had previously had a Gujarati-speaking volunteer who had now left.

Having a stronger funding base meant that some groups could offer a wider range of social and educational activities and advice. For example, a Jewish Deaf organisation, which had been in existence for over 40 years, had a resource centre with a range of special aids and equipment for Deaf people and a day centre for its elderly members. The organisation also published a quarterly magazine and provided welfare help.

Joining a group of this nature provided many deaf people with a chance to explore their culture, religion and also their deafness in an environment in which they felt comfortable. For some, it was the only opportunity they had to relax in the company of other deaf people from the same cultural background – which particularly appealed to those younger Deaf people who were experiencing communication problems with other family members.

The larger social groups also allowed the younger members to meet older deaf people of the same background, an opportunity they otherwise would not have had. This was appreciated as an opportunity for cultural socialisation and learning about appropriate gender roles and culturally appropriate expectations. One 17-year-old Pakistani student who regularly attended a women's group always looked forward to meeting older deaf women:

> "... I feel that I can learn more from older women because I am a young girl, so how will I know what it's like to be an older Asian women who is married or something? This is the place where I get an opportunity to understand and talk with them."

Indeed one social group, initially for Asian Deaf adults, had to rethink its membership when the organisers were approached by parents of deaf children asking whether it would be possible for their children to join. Involving young people in groups of this nature was seen as instrumental in developing their ethnic and religious identity, and introducing them to older deaf role models. The involvement of older Asian Deaf people served to show parents and children the capabilities of Deaf people and also the work opportunities that were available. According to one Indian woman in her early twenties, one of the reasons why the Deaf women's group she attended had been so successful at instilling confidence in members was that it was run by an Asian Deaf woman whom members regarded as a role model and with whom they could identify:

> "... to see role models that's very important. I mean, if it's hearing people teaching you all the time it's not going to work but if you've got a deaf role model there it's much better."

The absence of deaf role models was perceived as a problem particularly for African Caribbeans and some other ethnic groups. This had motivated a young African Caribbean Deaf student to set up a Deaf group, which had now been running for two years:

> "I want to see black [African Caribbean] people being proud of themselves. At the moment there are very few out there. It would be lovely if [Deaf] people out there could look at other black Deaf people and think 'I want to be like that'."

Deaf adult role models were thought to be a good way of presenting positive images for the younger deaf people. Within the social groups, it was felt to be important to have minority ethnic deaf people in positions of power so that they could instil confidence in the younger members and with whom the younger people could identify. Minority ethnic deaf presenters (especially those working in television) were therefore highly regarded as role models.

However, although social groups were highly regarded by most, some young deaf people felt that ethnically segregated social provision was divisive. Despite recognising that these groups had developed partly in response to the perceived racist marginalisation, some still felt that there was a need for unity with other deaf people facilitated through mixed social groups where there was scope to learn about each other's backgrounds and experiences. Deafness was regarded as a more important aspect of their identity than ethnic or religious background. Interestingly, some of these young people also talked about the racism which minority ethnic deaf people experience in mixed deaf groups.

Building social networks

Both workers and members of deaf social groups from minority ethnic communities were keen to develop links with other social groups. Many had already visited other groups in different parts of the country to learn about their organisation; newer groups were particularly eager to learn from the experiences of the more established ones. A number regularly organised parties for religious and social occasions such as Diwali, Eid and Rosh Hashanah, which also offered the opportunity to get together with other deaf groups.

Not only were these groups important in terms of bringing deaf people from minority ethnic communities together, some were able to provide a learning environment in which members acquired new skills and interests. The courses varied from assertiveness and leadership skills to improving English language skills. Confidence building was regarded as a particularly important issue for Asian Deaf women who were perceived to have low expectations, as noted by an Asian Deaf counsellor:

> "I really think Asian women are very negative.... I think they feel like they're not good enough, they want a good education, they want to get a good job but I think they feel, because of the hearing way, you know, you see hearing people and you think, oh very professional, you know, doctors or solicitors, whatever different professions, and I think they feel they just can't do it because they're Deaf and because they're Asian really. I think a lot of the women are like that."

This, however, was far from universally true; in the course of our fieldwork we came across many dynamic and confident Asian Deaf women, some, like the Asian counsellor quoted above, working in professional jobs.

Such groups also allowed opportunities to learn about Deaf culture and facilitate a positive Deaf identity. For example, through one such group, young Indian deaf women became informed about their ethnicity and traditions as well as about Deaf culture. Having had an oral education, they knew little about sign language and the existence of a Deaf community. Far from being divisive, their involvement in this social group facilitated greater affinity with the white Deaf people, through an improved knowledge of and affinity with Deaf culture.

There was considerable variation in the level of involvement that members had in deciding how these groups should be run. In general, members were consulted about their needs and efforts made to meet these needs. The groups had been encouraged to establish management committees to enable them to control their own affairs. For example, a hearing Asian community development worker had successfully done this with an Asian Deaf group, and saw it as an important development:

> "I mean it's very good actually, because before I used to say, 'Come on do this', but now they're telling me, 'Come on, we want to do this', it's a change."

There seemed to be a general consensus among members about the kinds of activities organised for their respective groups but conflicts did arise. At times it was difficult to reach a conclusion on aims and objectives, or to reconcile different users' needs. For example, at an Asian deaf women's group of different ethnic backgrounds, languages and age groups, some of the younger women resented the time given to 'basic' information on health and other issues which was valued by older users. Some questioned the value of having such a diverse group:

> "A lot of Asian deaf women in the group need to know about information themselves because they never had an education themselves. If they get educated themselves they will know what information they want to look for, whereas with us, we are already educated so we know where to get information, so maybe there needs to be a different group for people like ourselves."

Tensions also arose because members used the group for different purposes according to personal biographies and needs. While one older married

Deaf woman, who had been using the centre for three years, found it useful to share problems and receive counselling at the group sessions, some younger members said that they would discuss their problems with their Deaf friends rather than the workers at the centre even though they knew a counselling service was offered. However, despite expressing these concerns, younger people found the opportunity to be with older Deaf and hearing people of their own background beneficial for a variety of other reasons, as discussed earlier.

Identity and cultural sensitivity: some service responses

Respondents felt that mainstream services had a large part to play in providing appropriate support. For example, professionals had a responsibility to help deaf children become aware and confident of their ethnic and religious background in addition to having a 'deaf identity'. Educational institutions, health authorities and social services departments were all considered to be catalysts for change in this area, but there was considerable room for improvement.

Several teachers of deaf children and young people, based in both schools and colleges for the Deaf, recognised that their services were not responsive to the needs of minority ethnic students. It was felt that white staff needed support and training to learn more about minority ethnic cultures and develop links with and learn from families. This lack of cultural understanding disappointed some minority ethnic students. A Pakistani Deaf student at a college was disheartened by the Eurocentric teaching:

> **"... they have no information about our religion or culture. Our culture and religion should be respected equally. There is no information here either for Asian students or for the others."**

This was seen as particularly worrying in residential settings where Deaf students from minority ethnic communities had limited contact with their own communities and little or no religious input from the staff.

Where schools had taken the initiative to employ someone to teach minority religions, there was a positive response from the children and parents. One Asian hearing young man, invited to teach predominantly Muslim children in a school for Deaf children about aspects of their religion, recalled how pleased the children were to be able to have regular contact with someone of their religious background who could discuss religion and culture in sign language:

"I was surprised, the kids were really happy, the kids were really happy to see an Asian face in the school. And you know, I really did enjoy it and there were all sorts of questions you know. Varied questions about diet, about food, about dress, 'Are we allowed to wear this? Can we wear that? Can we eat this? Can we eat that? Can we draw pigs? Can we touch pigs?' They can only ask questions at school so how can a Pakistani Asian girl who's 12, 13 ask a white, mid-30s, early-40s teacher from middle class about her home life? You know, she can't...."

Similarly, parental pressure on a service for the hearing impaired precipitated their efforts to set up a cultural awareness class for Bengali deaf children living in the locality. The classes took place at a secondary school on Saturday mornings and were run by a Bangladeshi tutor with the aid of a sign language interpreter.

The need for specialised services: counselling and interpreting

Many black Deaf people were keen to point out how mainstream services were not addressing their needs and identified clear gaps in services. Having inadequate access to trained, culturally sensitive, sign language interpreters and counsellors were two of the serious deficiencies highlighted.

Counselling

A number of young Deaf people felt that counselling had a role to play in helping them work through questions of identity. However it was considered that counselling services offered by social services departments were more appropriate for the majority culture and generally not responsive to their needs. White social workers were felt to have little understanding of the pressures and constraints on minority ethnic Deaf people, thus making their services relatively inappropriate for minority ethnic users.

Social workers with deaf people felt a need to provide 'cultural counselling' for their younger minority ethnic users. Asian young Deaf people were found to be particularly in need of such counselling; issues of language and communication as well as culturally appropriate behaviour including family formation were among the reasons for the distress. One young Deaf woman was concerned that mainstream service providers did not acknowledge that Deaf people from minority ethnic communities were subject to a range of distressing pressures. She had herself trained as a professional counsellor and was now offering advice to minority ethnic deaf individuals and organisations. She talked about her reasons for setting up a specialised service:

> "... white Deaf people, they have counsellors and they can sort of understand each other but I felt ethnic groups are different because of their culture and I felt it would need a Deaf Asian person to be able to understand this, to understand the difference in our cultures. I feel we're very, very different and now when I meet people I feel, you know, they find it a lot better to sort of express themselves because they see me as a good role model."

Sign language interpreting and communication

It was widely acknowledged that there was a shortage of BSL interpreters who were from minority ethnic communities and fluent in their mother tongue. Nine sign language interpreters, the majority African Caribbean, were identified as working either in a freelance capacity or employed by organisations working with Deaf people. There was an expectation that such interpreters would better understand the experiences of and problems confronting minority ethnic Deaf people. This expectation extended to situations even where they did not share ethnicity or spoken language with their users.

One African Caribbean interpreter recalled an occasion when she interpreted for a group of Asian Deaf women. She found their positive response pleasing considering that she was of a different ethnic background. She feels that what mattered to the women was not the fact that the interpreter was black, but that she showed an appreciation and understanding of their background and culture which the women considered important. Another African Caribbean interpreter talked about the 'natural rapport' with black Deaf people:

> "You walk into a room, a black Deaf person sees you and their face lights up, and it's like, 'Yes', and there's an automatic link that you have. It doesn't breach impartiality, but it's there."

Having worked with minority ethnic Deaf people for several years, this interpreter was in no doubt that it was better to use interpreters from the same ethnic background. Another African Caribbean interpreter commented:

> "I've observed someone [white] interpreting for a black client who [the client] was very restricted in her signing. When I took over, she suddenly seemed to let loose and express herself much more ... later she said to me 'Usually [white] people think I'm really angry but I'm not angry'. I thought to myself that she was not doing anything to indicate that she was angry. I have seen interpreters assume they [black people] are angry. It's like with hearing people when they [Deaf people] get excited [hearing] people think 'they're going to hit me'...."

Such ethnic differences in signing and code-switching between home and school have been noted in the US as well as in Britain.

Politicisation as well as empathy and cultural understanding were issues addressed by others. An African Caribbean interpreter spoke of her own politicisation as well as that of the deaf people with whom she worked. This resulted in pride in their ethnic identity and many regarded these interpreters as important role models. Equally, the interpreters felt that signs and cultural signifiers were not always picked up by white interpreters. The example of 'hot combs', used in the 1970s to straighten hair, which needed a sign, was given by the interpreter as indicating the cultural gap between white interpreters and African Caribbean deaf people. The use of the hot comb sometimes left burn marks on the neck and 'Deaf people notice that kind of thing'. People did not like constantly being asked about the burn marks from white Deaf people. Interpreters also felt a strong sense of support from Asian Deaf women because they knew signs for relevant food (such as samosas and chapatis) and distinctions between different Asian groups (such as Pakistanis or Indians). Some felt that racism experienced by minority ethnic deaf people and their families resulted in barriers to support and information. Equally, racism was reflected in the Deaf world through the use of offensive signs for cultural groups or practices.

It was recognised that African Caribbean and Asian people were under-represented in sign language interpreting and that little was being done to encourage more people from minority ethnic communities to train as interpreters. Minority ethnic interpreters, because of their rarity and the advantages they offered, were a much sought after commodity, as noted by an Indian trainee interpreter:

"I went on a course recently and somebody was Deaf there and said, 'Oh I didn't know there were any Asian interpreters in the country and oh, wow, wow, wow, I'll pass your name around,' sort of thing and somebody else had heard recently, was a friend of mine who went to do some work and was asked did she know of any Asian interpreters because they wanted to set up provisions for Deaf [people]...."

A number of African Caribbean sign language interpreters highlighted the fact that African Caribbean Deaf people were prevented from learning about their own heritage without realising it, all because no signs existed to explain behaviour and practices pertaining to their own culture. This is consistent with the views of African Caribbean Deaf people, as noted earlier, who also criticised the lack of resources available to them for cultural socialisation. This was regarded as less of a problem for Asian people whose 'cultural distinctiveness' was generally accepted within the Deaf culture. Similarly Jewish Deaf people resented that no commonly used signs existed for some of their festivals or customs.

Additional problems confronted people who used sign languages other than BSL. There was a need for more relay interpreting to improve communication between services and deaf people who had no knowledge of English or of BSL. Relay interpreting enables information to be translated from BSL into any other sign language. In this respect, one hard of hearing woman, who ran an Asian Deaf women's group, found that the women who used her group sessions used different sign languages which meant that she had to relay interpret to ensure that users could be involved in group activities.

To overcome the problems faced by signers who were more fluent in their native sign language but had no knowledge of BSL or English, namely Deaf recent arrivals and refugees, a number of courses were established to help with basic English literacy and numeracy, and to develop communication skills. Access to information was an important issue which educational institutions and service providers were now addressing. An example, is the 'New Start' course at the City Lit College in London with modules in maths, communication skills, English and computing. There was a small scale but useful network for Deaf people arriving in this country in the London area but we found little evidence of this elsewhere in Britain.

Conclusion

The evidence in this chapter paints a mixed picture. At a positive level, there is much welcome activity on a range of issues of concern to minority ethnic deaf people. That many of these initiatives are relatively new, indicates both recognition by service providers and assertiveness and organisation on part of minority ethnic deaf people and their families. However, worryingly, the evidence also shows continued problems of short-termism, relative lack of mainstream activity and initiatives being driven by committed individuals in services rather than developing on the basis of clear strategy or organisational commitment. Evidence for any major shift either in the mainstream Deaf culture or services is thin. This chapter, however, shows that much of the user-led activity centres around ethnicity, culture and religion; an attempt at reclaiming and cultivating identities often denied to many minority ethnic Deaf people who became immersed in the dominant 'Deaf culture'. It is also largely based around Deaf groups using sign language.

Chapter 6 introduces initiatives around language and learning and explores issues of communication between deaf people and their families.

Language, learning and family relations

Language and communication are essential vehicles for socialisation and full membership of the family and community. They are intrinsically linked to reproduction of religious and cultural values, having a close association with and giving meaning both to cherished beliefs and actions. Children learn about their culture and identity from a variety of sources: through routine exchanges and relationships between family members and between families, literature and the media, through contacts with peers, and often through differentiation of 'insiders' from 'outsiders' which may also be accompanied by hostility from and towards 'outsiders'. Home language provides a potent marker of personal and group identity and provides an essential link between generations, between migrants and the countries of origin, and between members of a community.

As Rex (1991) and others note, migrants tend to reproduce in the new country the institutions and structures which sustained cherished beliefs and behaviours, and which give individuals and groups a sense of identity. Religious and home language teaching provides a major means of cultural reproduction for minority ethnic communities, as discussed by Anwar (1977), Afshar (1994) and Modood et al (1994). These authors note that parents are concerned both about imparting deeply and dearly held beliefs and behaviours to their children and guarding them against, what they may regard as, damaging or contradictory external influences. A variety of institutions ranging from the family to places of worship, the minority ethnic media, religious texts, rituals, festivals, literature and culturally appropriate forms of entertainment help to construct, sustain and service identities. However, this is not to deny that minority ethnic groups do not experience social change (Modood et al, 1994; Ahmad, 1996). Many of these issues are explored in Chapter 2.

Where there is no common language between children and their families, and where this hampers deaf children's access to both familial and extra-familial forms of cultural exchange, they may struggle to acquire the values, skills and behaviour essential to a positive ethnic identity and to full membership of the ethnic community. Further, because of communication difficulties, they may obtain only a partial and, perhaps distorted, understanding of what is happening around them, as noted in Chapter 5. Access to routine family exchanges, as well as formal teaching on mother tongue and religious education may also be lost. Further, as discussed in Chapter 2, children's exposure to what many may regard as a 'white' Deaf culture from an early age may make their peers the more significant socialising agents. Parents may feel helpless against this, and yet both parents and deaf children may resent the lack of communication with family and wider community, and access to important minority ethnic social institutions.

These issues are the focus of this chapter. We explore, first, young people's views on language and communication and its implications for their ethnic identity, and how parents' language and communication choices are influenced by different factors. Second, we discuss a variety of activity with a central focus on enabling parents to improve their communication with deaf children.

Deaf children, language choice and identity

Deaf children born into hearing families often grow up in a home environment where communication with their family is difficult without a common language and where they do not have full access to what is happening or being discussed around them. There is sometimes a lack of awareness on the part of hearing family members about the needs of the deaf child. All too often deaf children are excluded from conversations and activities going on within the home, thus denying them access to one of the primary means of socialisation.

Interviews conducted with Deaf young adults, from a variety of ethnic backgrounds, revealed that as children many had felt excluded from joining in conversations between hearing family members. In retrospect, they felt this had been detrimental in terms of building up their confidence as well as their cultural and religious awareness. One young man said, "My father only ever pointed to things – such as food. That was our only communication".

A Bengali bilingual worker who was involved with mothers of deaf children found that in many homes she visited the situation had not changed:

> "... the kids feel isolated at home because they can't communicate with the rest of the family and you know when you are talking about something they don't know what they

are talking about and no one bothers to translate for them, that's how most kids feel."

A major problem for minority ethnic families with a deaf child – just as with white families – is often the lack of a common language in the family. This made it extremely difficult for a strong relationship to develop between parents who had little or no signing skills and their deaf children. This was something which was noticed by one lecturer through meeting parents of students from minority ethnic communities. She cited the case of a Deaf male Pakistani student and his hearing father. The father was using the annual review meeting as a rare opportunity to communicate with his son, using an interpreter, rather than to find out about his son's progress which was the purpose of the meeting. The father had little understanding of his son's capabilities but held strong views about his own expectations for his son's future. There was a basic lack of communication between father and son. This situation was in no way unique, and illustrated the problem in most families where communication either remains superficial or is carried out through one or two family members who acquire relevant skills: mothers and siblings often became the family's link with the Deaf family member.

However, parents do take the matter of mother tongue teaching and cultural socialisation seriously and it appears that professional attitudes, though still variable, are now more accommodating of mother tongue use with young deaf children than before. In families where it is the norm for parents to speak to each other and with the children in their mother tongue, one of the first decisions which needs to be made by the parents is which language to use with their deaf child; sign language, their mother tongue, English or, indeed, all three. These decisions can be difficult and are influenced by professional attitudes, available help and the parents' own views about language choice and what some may regard as inappropriate additional burdens (in relation to mother tongue teaching) on their children. Parents first have to choose between sign and spoken language and then, if any have opted for spoken languages, which spoken language (see Chamba et al, in press, for a discussion).

Many parents found peripatetic teachers of the deaf helpful in giving advice about language choices. Some concerned parents had been relieved to be told that it would do no harm to communicate with their deaf children in their mother tongue. For example, one Bengali mother with two deaf sons had found the advice from the peripatetic service to continue speaking Bengali with her children as well as starting English and BSL reassuring and helpful. Had she not received this information she would have communicated with her deaf child using informal signs, which were not shared by other people. Another mother recalled how she was initially confused about language choice but was reassured once she had discussed her concerns about maintaining some communication in Bengali with the peripatetic service. The shift in policy from discouragement to active encouragement of family language use was welcomed by parents.

Speech therapy and language development

Some interesting developments in speech and language therapy were also noted. Speech and language therapists play an important role with some deaf children and adults. They work mainly in the NHS and their work is with the assessment of language and communication in children and adults as well as with speech and language therapy and counselling. Some departments provide specialist services for deaf children and/or adults, providing peripatetic services through schools, for example. For most therapists, their role covers all people with communication disorders. This may include dysphasia following strokes or children with late speech development. Their role in working with deaf people has taken on a new significance with the increasing emphasis on cochlear implants. We discuss below their role in relation to children and adults.

The limited number of languages in which speech and language therapy was available also influenced parental decisions about the choice of spoken language. In cases where speech therapy was needed, problems arose if the language used with the pre-school child within the home was not English. Speech therapists were often faced with the dilemma of deciding the most appropriate language in which the child should receive speech therapy (the mother tongue, English or both), although in reality resources for speech therapy in languages other than English were extremely limited. A social worker highlighted these difficulties in relation to different lip patterns between English and other languages:

> "... the parents don't speak English and that's the biggest hurdle ... is the lip pattern is different, like the two children that's just been done, and his mother speaks in their own language at home with them, and at school the speech therapist's helping them in English...."

Fortunately speech therapy and audiological training materials in languages other than English are being produced in some Asian community languages. These are intended to provide a better indication of the speech capabilities of children who are more fluent in their home language than in English.

Speech therapists in Glasgow had set up a short course for Punjabi-speaking parents which was aimed to help them understand the auditory rhythmic training patterns of the language they spoke with their deaf child. The course was run with the aid of a community language interpreter but was felt to be of limited success due to its short-term funding and location at some distance from the parents' homes.

The developments in cochlear implants mean that speech therapists play a greater role with late deafened people. One initiative in this area was working with two Urdu speakers who had received cochlear implants. Two specialist speech and language therapists had been employed to work with people from minority ethnic communities on short-term funding. Other health authorities have employed specialist co-workers with bilingual skills. On the whole, development in this area is slow, with few staff from minority ethnic communities with the necessary language skills. This has serious implications for deaf people's ability to find support in the development of speech and communication in languages other than English – a point also noted by others (Chamba et al, in press).

Sign language for parents

We identified considerable and varied activity around helping parents communicate with their deaf children, particularly through sign language or sign-supported English, but also through greater awareness about deafness. This activity ranged from formally organised, top-down 'teaching' to self-help groups facilitated by a tutor but which had a management committee and some autonomy about activities. Common to all these groups was the focus on communication with deaf children.

In the projects with whom we had contact, the emphasis was on enabling parents to use sign language with the deaf child in the home setting. To enable parents to develop sign language skills as early as possible, a number of education authorities and social services departments had set up sign language classes aimed at parents from minority ethnic communities. Some were targeted at parents whose first language was not English; others were open to everyone and made specialist provision for non-English speakers by employing bilingual support workers. In fact, sign-supported English speech rather than British Sign Language was being used in these classes, nearly all being taught by hearing tutors (see also Chapters 5 and 6).

On the whole, classes were attended by mothers, despite service providers encouraging both parents to learn sign language. In response to a preference for segregated classes, some authorities had organised separate sessions for males and females but found that, even then, fathers rarely attended. Reasons were offered by an Asian teacher and an Asian social worker. The teacher remarked:

> "Most fathers go to work, it's mums. Mums got the most burden I think. Mothers go out to learn to sign to communicate, whereas dad just uses basic gestures and signs to communicate."

The social worker added:

> "I found that with Asian men, they are not very interested really to do anything, yeah, anything with the child really, it's just the mothers really."

Benefits of sign language classes

Mothers found a variety of benefits from these classes. These included social support and help with understanding and coping with the child's deafness, in addition to learning sign language. For example, a young Pakistani mother found it comforting to meet mothers of other deaf children at the group and to share experiences of bringing up deaf children. She recalled how much more informed, supported, and at ease she felt having joined the group:

> "I never knew if there was deaf kids when I heard about my daughter, then you see other people's kids and everything, so it's really good to know other people as well and you get to know how they feel and everything."

Another Pakistani mother with two deaf children had similar feelings:

> "I was sat at home, just getting worried so I thought that I'd meet other mothers in a similar situation to myself. Sat at home you think you are the only one with a problem but when you venture outside the home you find that you're not alone, you find out about a lot of things. You find out that there are a lot of other people in a similar situation."

This mother felt that by joining the group she had found out about a lot of issues relating to deafness which she would not have picked up from elsewhere. It had helped her come to terms with her children's deafness and made her realise that others shared her concerns about bringing up a deaf child. She felt that these weekly meetings helped to put things into perspective and provided an outlet for mothers to share their concerns and worries. These views were shared by most other users of such groups.

The teacher running this group recalled a recent incident which illustrated how successful the group had been in providing a warm and supportive environment for the mothers:

> **"... there was a lady last week who actually felt able to talk to someone who she hadn't spoken to before about her children and she broke down and cried and they supported each other."**

Support groups and sign language classes were not only useful in bringing parents (largely mothers) together to learn and talk about their children's deafness, but also helped them to develop personal friendships outside the groups. However, there was a recognition among some service providers of the need to encourage the wider family such as siblings, grandparents, aunts, uncles and cousins to learn to use sign language to avoid the situation where mothers became 'interpreters' for the deaf children and for the rest of the family.

Not all groups had thought through how information should be transmitted to sign language class members. Materials were sometimes produced in English without considering whether mothers could read or understand them. Including mothers in decisions sometimes meant using community language interpreters working in conjunction with the sign language tutors. This facilitated greater interaction within the group and reduced the risk of misunderstandings.

Some tutors who ran sign language classes were keen on providing mothers with a written translation of the signs which they were teaching to enable them to share this information with other hearing family members. An Asian teacher of deaf children, who also ran a signing class, was keen on providing mothers with learning resources they could use at home. She produced a sign language video consisting of commonly used phrases with a voice over in Urdu, Punjabi, Bengali and English so that all the mothers attending the group could make use of it. Parents found such resources to be helpful. For example, a Pakistani mother with four children, one of whom was a seven-year-old deaf boy, found that by bringing written information home, her daughters and husband could learn signing and they could communicate as a family with their deaf child. She described how this was achieved:

> "In the evening after we've eaten we all sit together. My
> daughters, my youngest son and my husband ... and we relate
> to him, using signs, where we've been, what we've bought
> and we try hard to get him to talk as well as use signs."

In fact what she was describing was using sign-supported speech where
she was also using the sign language as a vehicle for teaching speech.

Poor communication had led to confusion and misunderstandings and
made routine childcare much more difficult. For example, a young Bengali
mother of a five-year-old girl was beginning to feel frustrated and helpless
at not being able to communicate with her daughter:

> "Sometimes in the mornings, she doesn't want to get up and
> you can't tell her you have to get up and you have to go, and
> she's really difficult. With a normal [hearing] child you can
> give them a shout but with her you can't, even if you scream
> your head off. You can't express yourself enough through
> sign because you don't know enough ... she ends up screaming
> and I end up putting her clothes on and things. Every morning
> it's the same story."

She felt that the situation would only improve through acquiring sign
language skills and had consequently joined a local support group where
sign language was taught.

Interest in sign language served both immediate and projected needs.
Parents felt that learning to sign at a relatively early stage would enable
them to meet their children's changing needs as they developed. This
included teaching on religious and cultural issues, an area which troubled
many parents. Without improved communication with their children,
imparting religious and cultural values was regarded to be difficult. This
mother found the situation upsetting:

> "He sees us reading the Quran, he sees us practise our religion,
> he sees us pray, he sees the other kids going to the mosque
> and he asks us why we are doing all these things but how can
> we explain it all to him when he can't hear? We feel it more
> now that he asks when we are fasting [during Ramadan], he
> asks 'Why aren't you eating your dinner?'"

Once parents started attending sign language classes there was little chance
that they would lose interest or feel that their needs were not being satisfied

(but note the limited involvement of fathers). Despite initially expressing a strong preference for their deaf child to use speech as opposed to sign language, many parents began to recognise the importance of sign language for their deaf child. One Asian teacher of the deaf who had set up a support group within her school felt her job was made much easier when parents were willing to acknowledge the benefits of signing and did not hold unrealistic expectations about their child regaining hearing:

> "... it takes a while before you can see results [from using sign language]. I mean, that's what convinces parents. I can talk until I'm blue in the face, but when you go home and you say, 'orange' or you say 'milk', you sign it and the child says 'yes' or 'no' or signs it back to you, you know we're half way there. I've won the battle as it were, because I don't have to convince them any more that sign is important, they know, their child is using it."

Sign language classes were also seen by professionals as an ideal opportunity to educate parents about wider issues relating to deafness and deaf awareness and deal with any concerns that they might have. Service providers felt that parents had much to learn about looking after a deaf baby and understanding its needs; their limited ability in sign language compounded this difficulty. One teacher of the deaf felt that many Asian deaf children would have benefited from greater stimulation from an early age:

> "They don't have any eye contact when they come here, they come looking somewhere else and you're signing.... I'd like, as I said, for children who will be coming into the nursery to have some knowledge of sign, preferably using it. I mean, I'm not talking about having a sophisticated conversation, but I'd like them to know about milk and orange and toilet, all the things that a two year old or a two and a half year old hearing child would know. Mummy and daddy and whatever...."

The mothers also used many of the weekly sessions to talk about any problems or queries they had regarding their child's welfare, including paperwork and benefits advice, as noted by an Indian social worker:

> "... they bring all their problems, mostly they bring a lot of letters because they don't understand, they might get a letter

from the school, they might get it from DSS, they might get it from, you know, various places, or even, you know, the Disability Living Allowance forms. I help them to fill them out, so that's part of the things that I'm doing with them mainly, you know, all the things, anything, the letter, the doctors appointment."

User involvement in sign language classes

The level of involvement that mothers had in deciding how sign language classes should be organised varied considerably. There was a general feeling among professionals that mothers were not assertive about the role of these classes. For example, a white teacher of the deaf, running a support group helped by a bilingual worker, illustrates this:

"What we haven't yet got is a lot of initiative coming out of the group on things they want to do, they're still quite accepting, you know, you give us what we need and we'll go along with it and I'm trying to make it so that, say what you want and we'll try and get you to provide it, but we're not at that stage yet and they're still quite passive yet really."

She recognised that the group was still in its infancy and that it would take time for mothers to gain enough confidence to start making demands on the service. However, with time some groups were becoming assertive in identifying their own needs and taking decisions. This is illustrated by the example of an Asian parents' group who, although initially passive, were now taking decisions about the group's work, as noted by the worker:

"It took about a year and a half for that carers' group to take the responsibilities, because I used to come every month and sit with them and say this is what [you should do], then I realised, 'No, this is it, now you have your committee, you tell me what you want, you tell me how you feel, this is your group not my group'."

A significant feature of the sign language classes we made contact with was that, in all cases, arrangements were made to transport mothers to and from their homes. This was valued greatly by mothers, some of whom would not have attended the classes as regularly had they been expected to make their own way. We return to this in Chapter 7.

———

Conclusion

This chapter has explored a number of debates around communication between deaf people and their families. That both deaf people and their families take the issue of language and communication seriously is clear from the evidence. The lack of a common language in the family which allows full participation by the deaf child in family life was recognised by all – deaf young people, families and professionals – as a major problem to be confronted. Language choice between BSL, English and other home languages was complex and affected by a range of factors, including personal knowledge and preferences on the part of parents, professional attitudes, available help and the degree of deafness. Some shift in professional perspectives was noted by parents; whereas once communication in the home language was seen as confusing and unhelpful for the deaf child, it was now often encouraged. Mothers were making an effort to learn BSL or sign-supported English and find out more about the Deaf culture, though fathers and other family members seemed absent from initiatives to promote such learning.

Chapter 7 explores organisational issues in developing and delivering services for minority ethnic deaf people.

Issues in developing services for minority ethnic deaf people

This chapter explores a number of interrelated issues: communication difficulties in accessing services; attempts to make services more culturally sensitive; funding mechanisms and their relationship to service development, user involvement and accountability; and developments in the voluntary sector. There is some overlap between issues discussed here and in Chapter 8; separation into two chapters, although not arbitrary, is largely for convenience.

Issues around language and communication are discussed in the opening section. These range from interpreting to information and services. Lack of interpreting provision remains a long-standing problem for sections of the minority ethnic population (see for example, literature on the Asian Mother and Baby Campaign – Rocheron, 1988; or for more recent work on nursing, Gerrish et al, 1996), and the distinction between interpreting and advocacy is often unclear. As noted in Chapter 3, sign language interpreting is regarded as distinct from advocacy and is guided by a strict professional code. Issues confronting users whose command of English is poor are explored by a number of authors and will be addressed in the discussion (Ahmad et al, 1989; Smaje, 1995). Secondly, we explore attempts at making services ethnically sensitive. Fashions in service delivery to minority ethnic communities change; the debates in relation to anti-racism and ethnic sensitivity are explored by Stubbs (1993), and we return to these issues at the end of the chapter. Thirdly, we consider funding for initiatives with minority ethnic deaf people. Funding plays an important part in the development of services, the relationship with users, systems of accountability and the degree of flexibility a service can offer. We discuss some of these issues and contextualise them in the wider literature (Atkin and Rollings, 1993; Atkin, 1996; Watters, 1996). Finally, we turn to the role of the voluntary organisations in relation to minority ethnic deaf people.

Language barriers

We found that mainstream service providers in health, education and social-care based settings had experienced problems in communicating with parents who had no knowledge of English. Where no provision was made for interpreters, it was often the case that English-speaking relatives were expected to interpret, but this was considered to be highly inadequate by both professionals and users, as noted by a teacher in relation to social gatherings attended by Asian mothers of deaf children:

> "... we would use mother tongue speakers from the various communities, somebody's sister-in-law and what have you and that wasn't satisfactory, because you were dealing with issues that maybe the mothers didn't want them to know what they were talking about ..., so we would then beg and borrow support workers from other Asian services ... but it was in no way successful."

Often service providers would depend upon the English-speaking father to translate information to his wife but there was never any guarantee that either of them fully understood the information which was being conveyed. It also depended on fathers being around to provide this service.

There were also reservations about using community language interpreters with parents of deaf children. It was felt that because these interpreters did not have any background knowledge of deafness, they would sometimes handle emotional situations without the required sensitivity. Some services employed bilingual staff with previous experience of working in the field of disability. This meant that they were more aware of the kinds of problems facing parents of deaf children and were therefore in a better position to explain disability issues in relevant languages. Service providers felt happier about the channels of communication once the language barriers were overcome and more confident that the information was being understood by parents, as is illustrated in the following example. A hard of hearing service manager talked about the benefits of employing a member of staff who was fluent in Urdu and Punjabi and could explain things effectively to the Asian mothers using the service:

> "... it was somebody ... who could tell them in their own language, what we were trying to get at. Why we were trying to get them to do these things, to play with prams and sweeping brushes, on the floor, and pretending to be something else. I think they just thought it was a bit of a joke you know. And

**we couldn't get through because of the language barrier ...
it's been wonderful to see the difference."**

Involving mothers in this way through improved communication was seen
by workers to be a positive achievement which encouraged better use of
services, appropriate care of the deaf children and allowed parents' needs to
be known. The head of the service felt that Asian parents, like most parents
of deaf children, were in a state of bewilderment following diagnosis and
recognised that there was a need for greater interaction between teachers
and parents to support parents with information, resources and guidance
on entitlements.

Not being able to communicate in English meant that some parents of
deaf children had little access to information, which also created problems
in accessing health and social services. This extended even to services
provided by bilingual staff when parents had to go through an English-
speaking receptionist. There was also a growing recognition that written
information needed to be produced in a more accessible form for deaf
people from minority ethnic communities and their families.

However, the employment of one or two workers did not always
overcome the difficulties. Lack of accessible information often remained a
problem, and parents' ability to make informal decisions about their deaf
child's care and language choices remained limited. This was important
around the time of diagnosis. Parents were also perhaps not in the best
state to understand complex information at a time most found stressful and
upsetting.

The feelings of shock, disbelief and powerlessness faced by many parents
around the diagnosis served only to exacerbate the already poor
communication due to language difficulties. Some providers were using
translated materials to help improve information exchange. An audiology
department was in the process of translating an information booklet for
parents of deaf children as part of its strategy to provide a fairer service to
all its users.

This problem of conveying information in a clear and accessible form
was not confined to parents of deaf children. Service providers in both the
statutory and voluntary sectors felt that older deafened and hard of hearing
people from minority ethnic communities needed information and support
in their own language on services and the use of hearing aids. The audiology
department mentioned above was in the process of translating information
into a variety of community languages relating to the effective use and care
of hearing aids.

In general, however, decisions made to translate information were based on the availability of funding and commitment among managers to provide a more accessible service.

Providing culturally sensitive services

Communicating in the same language was only one of the hurdles to overcome as part of providers' efforts to offer a more appropriate service to minority ethnic deaf people and their families. Many service providers in the statutory sector felt the need to know more about the cultural attitudes towards deafness and disability held by minority communities. Some also felt inadequately trained to deal sensitively with clients from ethnic minorities; lack of a shared language as well as limited cultural understanding were the main reasons for this. Deaf people from minority ethnic communities themselves also felt services to be insensitive:

> "I know Asian people have asked social services for better services and said that there's not enough but they sort of seem to withdraw from it and the service, I feel, is becoming worse. I think social services really need to become aware of the needs and rights of minority groups."

This view is echoed by a mother of a deaf child:

> "The social services are very terrible. Everyone is fed up of them ... the social worker says if you get something don't tell anyone else you are getting it [to keep down demand]."

One response to this perceived poor service and lack of cultural awareness was the employment of bilingual staff. A white manager of a social work department came to recognise the need to employ an Asian social worker, as he felt that deafness was perceived more negatively among the Asian community than in the white population, and this needed to be addressed:

> "... they [white social workers] couldn't understand the culture of it, you know ... because first of all they [Asian families] didn't want to use the hearing aids, they were arguing about that, they wanted to hide their disability."

In the manager's opinion, what was needed was an Asian person with appropriate language skills and a knowledge of deafness to work with the Asian community on deaf awareness.

For many organisations which had successfully set up services for minority ethnic communities, the key had been to start at the grassroots level and gain an understanding of community attitudes towards deafness and disability in general. Many white service managers had acknowledged that it was highly inappropriate for staff to impose Western ideas about deafness and Deaf culture and identity on communities who may perceive deafness differently. The emphasis was on understanding the communities' needs and organising services to cater for these. A young white deaf man who coordinated services to deaf people had learnt this from experience:

> **"If you try and start from the top and work down, it doesn't work. You've got to start from where people are at and then come back up."**

A willingness to listen to and respond to the communities' needs was felt to be crucial to success, as noted by a white manager of a Deaf centre keen to strengthen links with minority ethnic groups:

> **"It's not about giving people equal opportunity. It's about respecting people's cultures and beliefs and making the service fit in there. You can't actually go away, or go against, somebody else's beliefs and cultures ... it's not just saying 'Well here is a service. You come and use it'. It's about whether the service needs to change. Maybe it's better on a Sunday morning and not, not Thursday, or something."**

Indeed, it was due to this need to provide more appropriate services that minority ethnic deaf people and their families started to make demands on service providers in the statutory sector. This was noticeable in some social services departments and education authorities. For example, as part of its review of equal opportunities policy, one social services department became aware of the fact that its services were not providing equal access to the Asian community. Staff who undertook a survey on usership found that although deaf women were using the centre, only a small proportion of these were from minority ethnic communities. Successful attempts were then made to set up more appropriate provision specifically for minority ethnic women.

In places where specialist provision had been made for religious education for deaf children in schools, this had emerged in response to parental concerns. For example, at a deaf school with a large proportion of Muslim students with little knowledge of Islam, the impetus for change came from the community:

> "It was the parents putting pressure on the teachers or the school to provide something for their kids to learn about their cultural sensitivities, about their home life and things like that, respect of parents and all the rest of it and things like that. And also religious as well...."

Similarly, it was as a result of demands made by Bengali mothers of deaf children that an English class was set up by a hearing impaired service. These mothers were already attending a signing class but were conscious that they needed to improve their fluency in English to be able to learn more about their children's deafness. However, personal commitment of key professionals remained important in addressing parental concerns. It is doubtful, for example, whether this English class would have been offered without the support of the bilingual instructor who had developed a close relationship with the mothers and encouraged them to express their needs.

Within the voluntary sector as well, most initiatives had been set up by Deaf individuals themselves who were not happy with provision by mainstream Deaf clubs or by hearing organisations within their own communities. Some of these individuals had received both encouragement and practical advice from white workers in establishing such groups. It was felt that Deaf people from the Asian community were more successful in establishing such initiatives and securing funding. An African Caribbean Deaf activist was inspired by their efforts and was keen to initiate more social provision for African Caribbean deaf people using the same approach:

> "I think it's up to us to roll our sleeves up and say right we want services, if we see other people getting services it actually shakes us up, makes us want the same thing ... being involved in them ... it's important knowing that they're happening and passing them on the information."

Workers often had to manage tensions arising out of differing expectations of services. On the one hand, organisations had to ensure that they were providing services which were in line with criteria set down by the funding bodies to which they were accountable, and at the same time they were expected to act responsively to the needs of their users. Workers often felt caught in the middle and were routinely expected to reconcile these opposing demands if only to safeguard the future of the service. For example, an organiser of a hard of hearing group was told by her line manager that it was no longer feasible to provide members with free transport to and from the venue. However, the elderly users of the group felt the decision to be unreasonable and felt that they could not afford the travel costs themselves. The matter remained unresolved at the time of writing.

Problems regarding transport provision were also highlighted by a number of other voluntary groups. Limitations on the number of passengers meant that this service was available on a 'first-come first-served basis' which left the many potential users with no alternative but to use other means of transport, thus incurring additional costs.

Racism and difference

It was felt that minority ethnic deaf people needed to be more aware of equal opportunities issues and gain an understanding of how racist practices disadvantaged them in their daily lives. Nor was this an issue for minority ethnic people alone; many respondents felt that the white Deaf community needed to confront racism. Some of the more politically active Deaf people felt it important to expose and challenge the racist practices which they had witnessed, mainly in Deaf clubs. Among them was an African Caribbean youth worker who recalled the following incident:

> "There was one example in a Midlands Deaf club where a [black] person was discriminated against and banned for life which is terrible, but the white person had only been banned for six months and that made me really angry. I went into this Deaf club and told them that their attitude was all wrong in discriminating against this person and banning them for life and that they had left themselves open to being sued. The response was that I was not a member of that particular Deaf club and because of that very clever point I had to back off. I tried to explain what discrimination meant to the black members but they didn't understand...."

It was felt by many Deaf users that some Deaf clubs were treating Deaf people from minority ethnic communities as 'second-class' members and that some of these clubs were considered to be 'no-go areas' for non-white Deaf people. One young Asian woman in London who regularly attended an Asian Deaf group explained why she did not use her local club:

> **"Well, I've heard from people going there that it's a very white Deaf club so what's the point of going there if they're not very welcoming?"**

Accompanying the criticism of racism and hostility in the Deaf community was the charge of cultural insensitivity and an unwillingness to engage with diversity in the deaf world. This reluctance to deal with difference was echoed in one respondent's criticism of television programmes for the Deaf community. She felt that although efforts were made to include black Deaf issues there was also strong resistance to give too much coverage to such issues. The presence of an Asian Deaf presenter was perceived as very positive in Deaf broadcasting, before the programme was taken off the air. Minority ethnic issues were perceived to be marginal to the Deaf community's concerns and therefore not given sufficient coverage.

It was felt both by service providers and users that there was a lot of variation in terms of commitment towards equal opportunities issues among policy makers and organisations working in this area. Some users felt that too much emphasis was placed on the needs of deaf people as a homogenous, disadvantaged group with not enough attention being given to the experiences of minority ethnic people. However, within some statutory organisations, it was felt that there was often both a lack of understanding of equal opportunities issues or explicit policies; and that even when policies existed, there was a lack of commitment among staff to ensure implementation.

Funding considerations

For the majority of organisations and individuals involved in setting up and running services for minority ethnic deaf people and their families, funding was a major concern. Despite service providers having identified the need to set up specialist provision, funding these initiatives was an altogether different issue. Many of the bilingual support workers, teachers and social workers with the deaf people in the statutory sector were funded by local government Section 11 grants (now discontinued). Although this was a useful source of funding, its administration was not straightforward and restrictions were imposed on what the funds could be used for. For example, a manager of a Deaf centre with Section 11 funding for work with Asian deaf people had found that only limited developments could be paid for from this funding:

"With Section 11 money, that is only for services. Not for
things like car mileage, car allowances...or overheads. So ...
we will bring a member of staff into an establishment, it brings
with it overheads. The 'phone bill will go up. The training
budget goes up. You know, paperwork goes up, photocopying
goes up. All sorts of things. So I said to the social services
'well what about a support grant, is there any support grant'
to work those. 'Well, what money', you know, 'you have got a
worker', you know, 'be thankful.'"

Because of the funding difficulties, service providers sometimes approached
a number of different funding bodies in order to cover the costs of running
one particular service. This offered many advantages but often exacerbated
the difficulties of reconciling the varying expectations of different funders,
as well as responding to user demands.

For example, the funding for a support group for mothers of Asian deaf
children came from a variety of sources. The play worker, graphics designer
and transport were funded through a Single Regeneration Budget grant,
while the bilingual support assistant, who helped run the group, was funded
through a Section 11 grant. This pattern was repeated in funding for a sign
language class for Asian mothers, set up by a social services department.
While social services paid for the community languages interpreter, the
education department supplied the tutor and the library, and the leisure
department provided a grant for cultural activities such as small functions.
The funding for workers was always on a short-term basis with constant
pressure on the service manager to demonstrate the benefits of the service
to justify further funding. This created uncertainties for the service and
insecurity for the workers; it also diverted resources away from service
development and provision to monitoring and lobbying.

The lack of certainty about the future of services meant that long-term
development plans could not be devised and this led to a frustration among
workers, as noted by a service manager:

"... we've hobbled along from term to term, another term,
and another term, and it's always been, 'Yes maybe', 'But if'.
There is a rumour that this [funding] is being made permanent,
but I am not sure."

Within the voluntary sector, funding was considered to be even more of a
problem as individuals running services such as social groups were often
unaware of funding sources and inexperienced in acquiring funding.

Organisers were constantly on the look out for grants and ways of raising money especially to fund parties and cultural events. There was no guarantee that the same funding bodies could be approached again as criteria for funding were constantly changing and competition was fierce. Workers resented the considerable time and effort they spent on fundraising instead of developing services. They also felt, however, that without this the range and quality of services they could offer would suffer greatly. One young Asian hearing organiser of a voluntary group covered the running costs personally for a year until he became aware of potential funding sources. A major expense for the organiser was the cost of transporting members from their homes to the centre where the group met. This was seen as an essential part of the service by parents who were concerned about their children's safety while attending the weekly group meetings.

Some funding bodies placed certain constraints on activities which groups could organise, thus limiting the flexibility to respond to group demands. For example, workers at a deaf women's group who had secured funding from a local health organisation spent time with members talking about health-related issues. Other groups who had more autonomy over their budget had been able to set up services which were more in line with needs as defined by users and valued the flexibility such funding afforded them. For example, one hearing impaired service, having acquired a central government grant to set up a homework club for Bengali deaf youths, had also formed a much needed cultural awareness class for these children.

Sometimes workers made difficult compromises between funding remit and group demands. A community development worker who ran two deaf social groups, one for men and the other for women, was forced to merge the groups in an attempt to secure funding more easily. She felt that applying for funding for the two groups who were carrying out similar activities was confusing funders and hindering their chances of success. Members of both groups were consulted and the re-formed group agreed to share resources and decision making. They also decided to organise by gender as and when appropriate.

As a means of topping up their budgets, some Asian deaf groups had appealed to the goodwill of their own ethnic communities. Fundraising events to help cover the cost of organising parties and cultural events were successfully held by some groups and help was also secured from Asian businesses. Interestingly, one young hearing man who ran a group for Asian deaf youths was helped out by an Asian taxi driver who transported children at a discounted fare. One social group had been particularly successful in its fundraising efforts and had decided to set up a bank account in the group's name to be controlled by the members and used according to their needs.

Lack of funding had also held back attempts by a number of Deaf individuals from minority ethnic communities to organise conferences and workshops around issues of ethnicity and deafness. Many were already involved in voluntary sector projects and did not have the time or the energy to compete for funding. African Caribbean Deaf people also felt that they did not have adequate networks to keep them informed of funding opportunities and help secure funding. There was also an assumption among some service providers that African Caribbean Deaf people were less in need of targeted provision, which made their task of acquiring financial support even harder. This assumption rested on identifying needs in terms of religious and linguistic differences. As African Caribbeans were largely Christian and English-speaking, their needs were felt to be consistent with those of white deaf people. An African Caribbean Deaf woman pointed out the problem which rests on the perceived similarity between white and African Caribbean people compared to the perceived difference between white and Asian people.

> "Asian people have [different] religion, language, culture. If you asked an Asian person about their culture, they could tell you. If you asked a Black person, it's [perceived to be] the same as the white in a way if you think of it in those terms – they can go out, meet boys, go in clubs. Asian people can't, women only, different things."

A white social service manager made a similar point:

> "One of the things that we did find ... is that African Caribbean, those of African Caribbean heritage did not have a problem with youth provision ... the line was drawn in the sand between the Asian and the white."

The role of deaf voluntary organisations

There were widespread feelings among deaf people from minority ethnic communities that none of the mainstream deaf voluntary organisations were doing enough to support their concerns and interests. Many perceived there to be a lack of representation of minority ethnic people at a decision-making level within these organisations. However, efforts were underway to encourage the greater participation of minority ethnic deaf people and their families in events and activities organised by some of these organisations.

Deaf people from minority ethnic communities felt that these national organisations had a powerful role to play in educating the wider deaf community about issues relating to 'race', culture and aspects of discrimination – a task they were not taking seriously. A young Asian Deaf man who was active in promoting Deaf issues, but at the same time aware of his own cultural identity, was concerned about this neglect:

> "There's not enough about ethnic minorities and cultures. For example with the Asian culture, the prayers, the culture, Eid, the clothes, what it's like to be Deaf within an ethnic minority. We need to encourage much more publicity, the problem is, there just isn't enough. The Deaf, white community think, 'oh, Deaf people in an ethnic community is just like being in the white community', but it's not."

It was also felt that these organisations did not encourage minority ethnic Deaf people to participate in their activities. These reflected the needs of the white Deaf community and were often of limited relevance to Deaf people belonging to any other ethnic group. Not surprisingly, only a small proportion of the members of these organisations were from minority ethnic communities. The lack of involvement of African Caribbean people in national events was particularly conspicuous, as noted by a sign language interpreter of the same background who sensed that many African Caribbean people she came across felt resentful that too much attention was given to the needs of Asian Deaf people:

> "It's very sad really, at the BDA conference, you know, '100 Years' at Brighton, I saw a lot of groups, black people, signing away, but they refused to go into the conference. They just stood outside, you know, they just wouldn't get involved."

And these were the comments of another African Caribbean deaf respondent:

> "I'm certainly not objecting to white groups or Deaf clubs or white organisations like BDA or like NDCS – but personally I always feel the bottom of the pile all the time. Every time I go to places like that or courses I feel that I'm not given equal treatment."

At the 1996 BDA Conference, however, Asian and African Caribbean Deaf people were given a platform to discuss the problems they experienced in everyday life and the improvements they felt needed to be made, particularly in educational, health and family settings.

Voluntary organisations were generally criticised for the lack of support they offered to minority ethnic deaf groups in setting up forums to discuss issues relating to service provision and their own needs. Some of the organisations recognised that low representation of minority ethnic people reflected the cultural insensitivity of their services. Services needed to be made appropriate and welcoming, and this also required working with white users to ensure mutual respect, as noted by a representative of one large organisation:

> **"It's not that attitudes need changing because most of the people involved are quite willing to accept anybody with deaf children, it's really a matter of them being aware that there are different communities out there with deaf children and just increasing awareness really, especially for people who don't speak English ... and thinking about how activities are organised, who they're organising their activities for."**

Producing information in relevant community languages was one of the ways in which some of the voluntary organisations, particularly the RNID and NDCS, were making their services more accessible to non-English speakers. It was thought that much useful information was not reaching minority ethnic parents and that by translating their most popularly requested leaflets, they could help to increase parents' knowledge of deafness as it affected their child.

The voluntary organisations needed to promote their services to minority ethnic deaf people and their families and the wider communities in which they lived. This was felt to be particularly important for NDCS whose initial contact was with hearing parents, many of whom had a limited knowledge of the organisation's role. NDCS was seen as a powerful agency for promoting change in services and in some areas Asian parents were strongly advised to join NDCS groups as a means of campaigning collectively for issues concerning their deaf children's welfare.

Having minority ethnic involvement at committee level seemed to provide an incentive to other parents of a similar background to use NDCS. At the time of writing, NDCS has an officer with a particular remit to review minority ethnic parents' involvement and help develop means to enhancing their participation. However, some parents who were aware of NDCS and its activities still chose not to become members. The perceived stigma of deafness and a wish to cope within existing personal or family resources were offered as some of the reasons for the lack of involvement.

A white teacher of deaf children who was involved with a support group attended mainly by Asian women found this understandable:

> "I think at the moment people seem to be content with what they've got, because there is the feeling ... we'll keep this within our family, now we'll keep it within the community, now we'll keep it within this intimate little group ... as the children grow up through school, they have wider ranges of contacts and you'd hope NDCS would become one of those. 'Cos quite often it's the case that the children will choose to do something and then mum and dad will go along with them, really."

What seemed to be important was to make sure that parents were provided with information about services available through NDCS so that they were in a position to make informed decisions regarding their children's deafness. To this end, local representatives of NDCS had visited local support groups for parents of deaf children from minority ethnic communities to inform them about NDCS activities and, in turn, listen to the parents' concerns.

The BDA is also taking steps to encourage greater involvement of minority ethnic communities in its organisational activities. Money secured by their Deaf youth officer from the Rank Foundation to work with disadvantaged groups made it possible to focus on the needs of minority ethnic young Deaf people. Consultation meetings set up with Deaf youth in different parts of the country generated information for the BDA about their needs and the desire to set up separate groups with support from the BDA. These young Deaf people also expressed a desire to undertake training offered by the BDA in the areas of confidence-building and assertiveness as well as courses leading to formal youth work qualifications.

As a consequence of this consultation process, many groups had developed in different parts of the country which were headed by Asian Deaf youth workers fully trained by the BDA. The BDA is committed to continuing its work with ethnic minorities and especially with young people, as this is seen to be an important area with scope for further development.

Conclusion

Overcoming language barriers emerged as a significant concern for service providers. Issues included limited availability of trained interpreters, or interpreters who were knowledgeable about deafness and related services, problems of using family members for interpreting and difficulty in access to information. The related issue of ensuring ethnic sensitivity in service delivery was being addressed in different ways. This included, at times, the need to provide gender specific services or respect for cultural and religious sensitivities. We found much criticism of the major deaf organisations.

Finally, funding uncertainties created problems for workers and deaf users alike. In particular, there was a perception that funding was difficult to obtain for African Caribbean Deaf initiatives because they were assumed to share the same culture as white Deaf people. In contrast, the presumed cultural difference of the Asian groups advantaged them in competition for funding. These and related issues are discussed in Chapter 9.

Chapter 8 explores perspectives from workers on developing services for minority ethnic deaf people and their families.

Developing services:
the workers' perspective

This chapter extends the discussion presented in Chapter 7, beginning with an exploration of the issues confronting workers. These include training, networking and the different experiences of deaf and hearing workers. Secondly, we discuss what makes services 'user friendly', along with tensions created by attempts to be flexible within rigid project remits. Thirdly, some of the constraints experienced by users and workers are explored. Fourthly, we consider the support needs of staff in an environment often charged with racialised resentment from white users and colleagues. Finally, we look at the nature of interagency collaboration in providing appropriate services to minority ethnic deaf people.

Workers' experiences

Workers came from a variety of backgrounds with differing skills and levels of experience. Factors which affected the kind of worker appointed included where the service was based (statutory or voluntary sector) and whether it was part of a generic service or a specialised initiative. Generally, projects based in the voluntary sector, such as social groups, were established by minority ethnic deaf people who recognised a lack of service provision to address the needs of people like themselves. Such workers had little or no previous experience of running groups and were keen to acquire skills so that they could carry out their roles effectively. Services which were based in the statutory sector, however, were more likely to be run by hearing professionals, both minority ethnic and white.

Many statutory sector organisations felt that they needed to appoint someone who would enable them to improve their services, by providing cultural insights and developing closer links with minority ethnic deaf people and their families. Service providers who dealt with parents of deaf children felt that it was necessary to appoint someone with the appropriate community language skills to ensure parental access to information and services. In cases where bilingual workers had been employed to help parents to cope with the initial diagnosis of their child and the early stages of their school years, it had made a significant difference to the relationship between services and parents. For example, a white peripatetic teacher with a large caseload of Bengali deaf children had employed a hearing woman from the Bangladeshi community as a support worker within the hearing impaired service. This person would facilitate access to hearing impairment services as well as offer advice on other issues. By having such a person, it was hoped that the organisation would learn to offer an improved and more sensitive service to this group of users.

Part of the problem faced by this hearing impaired service was that of using different community language interpreters when talking to mothers of Bengali deaf children. Because these interpreters were not sufficiently knowledgeable about deafness, they would not necessarily convey information to parents in a consistent manner. By appointing a Bangladeshi woman who herself had experience of bringing up a deaf child, the hearing impaired service found that the parents were much more willing to talk to her about sensitive issues. The parents felt that the bilingual worker could understand and appreciate their cultural circumstances better and they felt comfortable in discussing their concerns with someone in their own language.

In another hearing impaired service, an Indian woman with the appropriate language skills had been employed to work with mothers of deaf children, the majority of whom were Pakistani. Despite not belonging to the same ethnic group as the mothers she was aware of the women's social and cultural circumstances and could appreciate their perspectives and experiences. Interestingly, having an Indian person to turn to was seen as a relief for the Pakistani mothers. It meant that they could share personal problems with someone who was not from within their own community and therefore afforded greater confidentiality and yet who had relevant language skills and cultural knowledge which the mothers valued. This was also commented on by an Indian social worker who was dealing with mostly Pakistani service users.

The language skills of these workers came in useful on various occasions such as when they had to accompany teachers of the deaf on home visits to families, when mothers needed help with interpreting at hospital appointments and in assisting deaf children in schools with language development. Social workers and support workers also played a role in setting up and encouraging mothers to join sign language classes.

Similarly minority ethnic social workers, employed to address the problem of low take-up of services, were expected to work closely with their communities to explore attitudes towards deafness and disability as a way of finding out about the problems faced by deaf adults and their families. Asian social workers made use of community organisations and the ethnic media to advertise services they had set up. Liaising with community groups and individuals seemed to be an effective way of generating interest in these new services.

In this way, for example, an Asian community development officer who had been employed to improve access to services for the deaf, visited various community centres and informed people what was on offer to deaf and hard of hearing people. It was only through talking to older Asian women that she found out that most of them did not consider having a degree of deafness to be a problem and therefore did not feel that they required her services. It clearly needed someone from within the community to elicit such information which proved to be important in explaining why take-up of services was low among this group of people

As noted earlier, in some instances it did not matter so much that the worker did not belong to the same ethnic background as the service users. However, it was important that the worker, whatever their background, showed an understanding of the cultural values of ethnic minorities and understood the way in which these influenced their lives. A white Deaf youth worker felt that her many years of training had given her the skills to work closely with Asian deaf people. She felt that trust, empathy and an understanding of disadvantage and discrimination faced by minority ethnic users was important for good service delivery. A few youth groups and sign language classes set up by white, hearing professionals put the onus on users to define how they wanted the service to develop and were keen to learn more about cultural issues from members.

There is an interesting trade-off between being deaf and being from a minority ethnic community, and of the appropriate gender, for workers and users. A hearing worker was sometimes seen as acceptable by a deaf group by virtue of being a member of a minority ethnic community while this may be unacceptable for a white hearing worker. Deaf-led projects which thrived seemed to be run by Deaf people, but there was still some discrepancy between minority and majority ethnic communities. In Deaf work with majority ethnic groups the orthodox view is that projects should be Deaf-led wherever possible. This seems to be less true of projects with minority ethnic Deaf people. Reluctance to accept a hearing person, however, even one from the appropriate ethnic group, was certainly not unknown, as was indicated by the following example of an Asian hearing worker who was initially disenchanted with her work:

> "… I used to cry, I said, 'Oh my goodness I want to leave' and
> my director said, 'No you're not'. I said, 'I have to leave, look
> at them', they used to treat me really badly because I was
> hearing. And the Deaf community is very close community."

There were fewer training opportunities for minority ethnic Deaf workers
compared to white Deaf people. Minority ethnic Deaf people were under-
represented in sign language teacher training, in education and as
professionals generally. However, youth work training is an area involving
larger numbers of minority ethnic Deaf trainees.

On the whole the workers did not regard their gender, ethnicity or hearing
to be a problem in carrying out their jobs, although we have noted divergent
views on this earlier. However, an Asian sign language tutor felt it would
have been advantageous for the group to have had a Deaf tutor. With a
hearing tutor who spoke the relevant Asian languages, the mothers tended
to slip into their own spoken language during the course of the class:

> "You are distracted from signs and you don't pick it up as
> well and that was what was happening, it didn't matter how
> much I sort of, you know, if I was talking about something
> that they didn't understand, I'd side step the gesture to try
> and get the point across. Err, but they'd always not watch, it
> was like, just tell me what you're saying and … I always felt it
> was more useful to have a Deaf person, because they couldn't
> resort to talking."

This last comment reflects the accepted practice of Deaf tutors teaching
sign language – a point stressed in the BSL teacher-training courses taught
at Durham University and City Lit Centre for Adult Education.

Provision of sensitive services

Workers found that it was not always possible to follow standard methods
of service delivery. More sensitive service delivery required some scope for
flexibility, especially as services were organised on white norms. Some
workers found they needed more time with each minority ethnic client
than that needed by white workers with white clients, as noted by an Asian
social worker:

> "… with English social worker, they'll go and visit the family,
> they'll just do an assessment, come back, they write the

equipment what they needed, that's the end of the story. Whereas in my case, if I go and visit a family, I do an assessment whatever, then there'll be a lot of information passing, there's a lot of questions they have to ask, there's a lot of, you know like filling the forms, they can't do it themselves, there's a lot of letters to tell, they get letters from school, they need to, want to know from me what's this all about, can you tell us what's this, what shall we do if this letter comes from school, can you find out more information for us because we can't talk to the school. So I, on their behalf, I'm doing a lot of work...."

Minority ethnic workers also had to guard against being marginalised. Those working at a senior level were careful not to be used as interpreters, especially when working with professionals from other agencies keen to extend their services to minority ethnic groups. This was an easy trap to fall into for minority ethnic professionals who recognised their own skills but felt that they were not qualified interpreters and that to be used in this way was an abuse of their job description. It was noted in Chapter 3 that there has been a gradual separation of sign language interpreting and social work over the last 10 years. Seeing the interpreter as a channel between two languages and allied to neither is still not widely accepted by users of interpreters and minority ethnic workers being used as ad hoc interpreters is a long-standing problem requiring attention.

Minority ethnic professionals also felt that many white colleagues assumed that having a specialist worker meant they did not have to develop their own competencies or practice. In the statutory sector especially, white colleagues were likely to turn to the specialist worker to deal with a range of problems experienced by minority ethnic users, resulting in these workers being overburdened with cases which no one else felt they were capable of dealing with. One social worker, for example, felt that this level of dependency on her was not good for the service:

"... they said 'oh I was having this problem with Asian child', you know, 'we couldn't cope and', you know, 'we wanted you there and tell us more about the culture and tell us more about the things, are we doing the right things."

Constraints on developing services

It was often the case that new roles had been created within organisations to address identified needs, but particular communities and workers were often frustrated at the lack of support and guidance they received when they set up a new service. Workers also felt that Asian families looked upon deafness in a different way to English families or confronted additional problems in securing necessary support. Not having independent access to information meant that there was greater dependence on the workers to explain aspects of deafness or access to services, which was time-consuming for the worker and potentially stressful for the parents. There was a greater likelihood of tensions between workers and management in cases where the latter did not understand these issues and were content to use the standard models of service delivery developed with the white deaf population in mind.

Workers felt constrained in their ability to respond to user needs which would mean changes to service organisation or had resource implications. An Asian social worker with deaf people recalled how, despite demands for counselling and a support group from the Asian community, her department was not willing to support these services. She described the scenario:

> "... our department couldn't understand why I'm spending more time with them, why I'm doing this extra so they were saying, no, just purely do work as a social worker and that's the end of the story ... so there was a lot of problems going at the work, and I really stood for them, I said 'Look, if you want my services, that's what I have to do'."

Other workers provided services which were linguistically more appropriate. A worker with hard of hearing and deaf people from one predominantly Gujarati community developed culturally and linguistically appropriate services, including lip-reading classes in Gujarati:

> "You're not going to expect people the age of 60 to learn English, there is opportunity for people to learn lip reading in English but that is going to be very different when you translate that word like 'pat', 'rat', 'mat', which sound very similar when you translate that 'pat' into an Asian language that will sound completely different and the pattern would be very different and I have tried where my literacy tutor, who's bilingual and she's a Gujarati speaker herself, but it did not work because there's different ways of doing things. So really there is a need to have that because there is not the provision here."

However, her desire to learn from possible developments in south Asian countries in this field remained unfulfilled because of the costs of the trip and replacement cover. Indeed it was important for workers to look at what could be achieved realistically given the financial constraints they were working under and the limited amount of support available to them.

Workers employed as part of a team felt it important to be able to suggest changes to existing patterns of service provision. However, many felt frustrated at the limited opportunity to affect service change and they felt that their ability to offer an appropriate service was compromised.

Struggling against organisational constraints was felt to have a heavy price for the workers both emotionally and in terms of tarnishing their reputations as potential trouble-makers who had little desire to be a 'team player'. This is illustrated by the experience of an Asian social worker who found her manager particularly unsympathetic to her demands to introduce sessions on a topic in which women attending her signing class had expressed an interest:

> **"I'm sick of now struggling all the time, sick of fighting all my life, I'm sick of telling people … and you think, why do I have to struggle all the time, why not others? And then once you're struggling and telling them people and you are the one, who becomes a bad person, you got that stigma all the time, 'she's the one who's always making a fuss, she's the one who's always saying things'."**

It was felt that managers needed to understand that what they defined as priority areas might not necessarily coincide with what the users considered to be important in terms of service provision to minority ethnic communities. For workers to have credibility with users, an element of flexibility and willingness to respond to user demands was regarded as important.

Lack of support

The problems and frustrations of trying to meet user demands with limited resources and/or skills, and with limited support from colleagues and managers, was a common theme in discussions with workers. Those working in an individual capacity without an organisational base felt particularly unsupported. For example, one Asian Deaf young mother felt under pressure in the early stages of setting up a women's group because members were expecting her to perform roles for which she did not have qualifications, skills or resources. She described how she became overloaded very quickly with unrealistic demands:

> "... women came to me with problems, problems, problems. They thought I'm a social worker, a knowledge[able] computer person. I'm not, I'm nothing, I'm a mother person. And they expect me to relay, to communicate [interpret]. I did a lot of work and all the problems ... telling me ... telling me ... and I became emotional and stuck. I've got no one to share it, nobody, so I get stressful very quickly."

This Deaf mother (quoted above) had no experience of facilitating a voluntary group, knowledge of funding sources or management experience. She felt that her job was made harder by the fact that she received no supervision for an entire year. This example also shows that the division between 'users' and 'workers' is often blurred in the voluntary sector, in that this woman was a mother of a deaf child who was keen to help others like herself.

The problem of isolation was not confined to the voluntary sector. Workers in the statutory sector also felt inadequately supervised and supported, with many commenting that there were underlying tensions between themselves and other staff working within the same department. According to some workers, some white colleagues (both deaf and hearing) felt threatened by the roles and achievements of these specialist workers and showed concern that resources were being channelled into 'ethnic minority causes' at the expense of other users.

White deaf users were often felt to share this resentment. The main problems were about the perceived preferential treatment of minority deaf people and the supposed divisive nature of organising separate provision. An Asian Deaf youth worker based at a Deaf club, for example, had set up a group for Asian Deaf people but experienced hostility from white users who felt that nothing was being organised for them and were reluctant to participate in activities organised by the Asian Deaf youth group. As a result, the worker tended not to discuss 'Asian' issues with white Deaf people using the centre as she felt this would lead to unnecessary tensions with the other workers as well as users. Being the only Asian on the committee of the Deaf club, she was careful not to 'rock the boat' and was keen to involve more Asian deaf people on the committee so that they were in a better position to make their demands known. She described white members' resentment:

> "... they were saying 'Why have you got something special for this group?', you know. 'Why don't you come and play with us?', you know, and 'Where is all this money coming from.

You can get money for them, but you don't get money for us'. That, that has created problems. There is always bits of money for ethnic minority work. You can get that. You can set up a an adult literacy class for Asian women, but you can't do it for white Deaf women. And it has created a bit of a tension there, you know...."

These tensions also arose when an African Caribbean youth worker discussed his intentions of setting up a social group with his colleagues and received no encouragement:

"... white people did criticise me for wanting to set up this and asked if I meant to divide white and black people. I explained that that was not what I meant. Nobody supported me, nobody, so I felt that I had to keep mum about the whole thing."

Importance of networking

Given that a number of workers felt isolated and unsupported, and often experienced resentment on the part of their white service users, it is not surprising that some had developed links with workers in other parts of the country. Apart from providing valued support, such networking was thought to be beneficial to learning about service developments in other localities and exchanging information and advice. It was felt that workers needed to meet on a regular and formal basis so that managers would be more likely to give the meetings some credibility. Attempts had been made to establish a national forum, but lack of support from managers made it impossible to sustain this national network.

Examples of interagency collaboration

Workers were also keen to promote awareness among other service providers of the particular needs of deaf people from minority ethnic communities. Many had developed collaborative work with colleagues from other agencies. The strongest links were between health professionals dealing with young deaf children and peripatetic teachers working for hearing impaired services. It was common for teachers and their bilingual support workers to be heavily involved in assessing hearing and language development. In the case of families with a deaf child whose first language was not English, bilingual support workers usually accompanied the teacher and in some cases visited families on their own. Intervention at an early stage was felt to be important as it gave parents the opportunity to learn about deafness and the child's language development needs.

In one London borough, a multiagency approach between professionals in health, social services and education was being developed so that areas of common concern regarding deaf children from the predominantly Bengali population could be highlighted and addressed. One concern related to problems in diagnosing deafness among Bengali children. Children with moderate to severe hearing loss were often not being detected until as late as seven years old. This was causing distress for parents who were having to come to terms with their child being deaf without the required support and advice. The one peripatetic teacher employed by the hearing impaired service in this borough had been instrumental in recruiting some members of the Bangladeshi community to provide support to Bangladeshi families with deaf children. She also liaised with health and social services to facilitate a coordinated service.

Where social work departments had employed ethnic minority staff, they were sometimes called upon by health professionals to advise on culturally sensitive service delivery. Equally, in social work departments where staff felt that they were unable to resolve the problems facing their minority ethnic deaf users, they were likely to refer these people to specialist groups or workers who provided counselling and advice services.

One Asian Deaf women's group had consciously developed links with the local social services department so that social workers were aware that the group existed and would refer cases which they felt workers at the group were in a better position to deal with. The organiser of this group, an Asian Deaf woman, did not feel that the white social workers would fully understand the cultural circumstances of the Asian Deaf users and felt that she had the skills, background and experience to offer a culturally sensitive service.

It was not always the case, however, that agencies took up the opportunity to work collaboratively, even when they were aware that specialist services or staff existed. For example, a school for deaf children serving a large number of Pakistani Deaf students did not wish to develop formal links with a local Asian Deaf youth group even though the school had played a part in setting up the group in response to demands from parents. Although staff were prepared to promote the activities offered by the voluntary group among their students, they preferred the group to operate independently from the school. In effect this meant that it was left to the hearing volunteer to organise funding and a venue for the group in order to cater for the educational and religious needs of local young Asian Deaf people.

Another example was of an audiology department where a Punjabi-speaking patient had received a cochlear implant. Problems arose once the rehabilitation programme began as the department had overlooked the fact that the patient needed speech therapy in her home language rather than in English. The patient at that time had contact with a Punjabi-speaking social worker who was willing to work with the patient but the audiology department dismissed this offer. Instead they decided to employ a speech therapist from Pakistan to work with the patient for a two-year period. This proved unsuccessful, however, as the speech therapist spoke a different dialect of Punjabi to the patient and then returned to Pakistan sooner than expected.

Conclusion

Issues addressed in this chapter overlap with those discussed in Chapter 7. There was a greater involvement of minority ethnic deaf people as providers in the voluntary sector and a greater involvement of hearing minority ethnic professionals in the statutory sector. Those in the voluntary sector remained poorly trained with little prospect of acquiring qualifications or secure employment. In terms of ensuring sensitive services, the need for flexibility was particularly important, but there was a perception that current health and social care structures worked against this. The minority ethnic workers often lacked support networks and at times worked within an atmosphere of racist hostility from white Deaf users and colleagues. Finally, there were few examples of good cross-agency collaboration; the boundaries across health, education, social services and the voluntary sector made effective collaboration difficult, although not impossible. However, there were some examples of effective collaboration between education and health services.

We discuss the findings from this and earlier chapters in Chapter 9.

Minority ethnic deaf people and service initiatives: a discussion

This was an ambitious project, aiming to provide a national overview of initiatives on ethnicity and deafness. We examined a wide range of initiatives: in the statutory and the voluntary sectors; established and fledging; large scale and relatively modest; financially secure and minimally funded; in major cities and smaller localities; focusing on different user groups; and both Deaf-led and organised by hearing people. The work represents the first major overview of such activity in Britain, although earlier work has been of considerable value (Sharma and Love, 1991; Badat and Whall-Roberts, 1994), and some recent work offers more detailed accounts of services for children (Chamba et al, 1998). Below we discuss the main findings and set these in the context of relevant literature and debates on ethnicity and social policy.

Focus and location of initiatives

A common characteristic of many of the initiatives was that they did not form part of a well thought-out strategy for improving service provision to minority ethnic deaf people. Short-termism, separation from mainstream services and precarious funding are all common features of 'specialist' provision to minority ethnic communities (Anthias and Yuval-Davis, 1993; Atkin, 1996; Watters, 1996) and are shared by initiatives in this area. Consistent with what we know about service provision to minority ethnic groups generally, many initiatives depended on the personal commitment of individuals and thus did not reflect, and were not always intended to lead to, a cultural change in the way in which their organisations interacted with minority ethnic clients. Watters (1996) explores similar issues in relation to initiatives on mental health. This, fortunately, was not a universal phenomenon, and the exceptions showed what could be achieved through a well planned and appropriately resourced strategy: the example of the Fosse Health Trust in Leicester (discussed in Chapter 4), among others, is significant in this respect. It is important to acknowledge also that initiatives need not be expensive to achieve success; the decision by two audiology departments to provide hearing aids in tints which more closely matched the users' skin colour (rather than the conventional pink aids) shows that a level of ethnic sensitivity can be attained without additional resources.

The initiatives show an uneven development. They are largely concentrated in major cities with relatively large minority ethnic populations, and there is little activity in smaller cities and rural areas. This is consistent with developments in the area of ethnicity and mental health (Leicester Black Mental Health Group, 1988), haemoglobinopathies (Ahmad and Atkin, 1996a) and minority ethnic-led housing (Harrison, 1993). However, the implication of uneven development between large centres and smaller towns is that users in the latter will experience even greater isolation and less sensitive services. The experience of testing for industry-related deafness in Bradford was that many users came from outside of Bradford and had found out about the service from friends or relatives. Similarly, Li (1992) notes that because of the lack of facilities aimed at the Chinese population, specialist centres such as the London Chinese Health Resource Centre attracts users from great distances.

Two major concerns are apparent in terms of the focus of most initiatives. One is the emphasis on 'special needs'. Many of the service-led initiatives provide information and help with communication, make available resources in languages other than English, provide interpreters and produce minority language videos about deafness or services. Such initiatives are important, as literature on minority ethnic communities and welfare services notes poor access to information and problems in communication (Shah, 1986; Patel, 1993; Butt and Mirza, 1996; Johnson, 1996). Yet this approach reflects the reductionism of earlier responses to other areas of minority ethnic needs where needs are reduced to people's presumed cultural difference (see Ahmad, 1993, for a critique). Also, few of these initiatives employed deaf people from minority ethnic communities – the picture was one of hearing workers with BSL skills providing services to deaf people and their families. The minority ethnic deaf people were relatively rarely seen as providers in the statutory agencies, although they are beginning to emerge in professional roles.

An important development was the provision of BSL or sign-supported English to parents of deaf children. Interestingly most such classes were used by Asian mothers – Asian fathers and learners from other minority ethnic backgrounds were less commonly seen in such classes. This may reflect the greater involvement of mothers with their deaf children and hence their greater need for such provision or the relative inaccessibility of classes to fathers because of timing, cost or transport.

The second focus is on issues regarding ethnic and religious identity – a concern shared by professionals and minority ethnic deaf people alike (for parallels in relation to disability, see Stuart, 1992 and Begum et al, 1994). Identity politics acted as an important organising principle for many of the initiatives, especially the social and cultural groups organised by Deaf people themselves. Ethnic and religious identity was important for minority ethnic, especially young, Deaf people and many felt that the immersion in a 'Deaf identity' had not afforded them access to these other, vital aspects of their heritage. That much of the social activity was organised on an ethnic/ religious (and often also a gendered) basis shows the importance of ethnicity and religion as markers of selfhood. This was particularly an issue for younger Deaf people and recognised by themselves, by older people from minority ethnic communities and by service professionals. The negotiation of Deaf identity in relation to ethnic/religious aspects of selfhood was a major concern for the younger people but not for older hard of hearing and deafened people. We return to this later.

The 'specialist worker' syndrome

As noted, many of these workers were hearing minority ethnic people based in statutory agencies. Their predicament has parallels with what is generally known about specialist workers (Ahmad, 1993; Alladin, 1992; Watters, 1996), one common problem being that of 'dumping'. Waseem Alladin, a clinical psychologist, recounts his personal experience in this regard:

> 'This one is for you, Waseem!' When a black patient is referred, somehow it is held that I am an authority by virtue of the colour of my skin, irrespective of the problem being presented. While I value white colleagues who recognise their limitations (as I recognise mine), I would prefer that they join with me in seeing black clients so that together we may learn how best to deal with those who do not share our own cultural beliefs. (Alladin, 1992, p 134)

There are clear problems with 'dumping'. One is that the 'specialist worker' becomes the minority ethnic users' main contact with the organisation so that they may end up with access to a smaller pool of expertise. Related to this is the often lowly position of 'specialist workers' which may also disadvantage their clients. Second, 'specialist workers' often become the visible social conscience of their organisations. Rather than being signifiers of the commitment for positive change, they somehow absolve the organisation from any need for a shift in attitudes or practice. Thirdly, as Alladin notes, white colleagues remain impervious to the need to change their own practice or to acquire new skills to enable them to deal with minority ethnic clients more sensitively. Finally, 'specialising' on minority ethnic clients hampers the 'specialist worker's' chances of operating with a broad client base, and thus may affect their career prospects. This is not to deny that having specialist workers can be of benefit to minority ethnic clients, or to the employing organisation (see Atkin et al, 1997, in relation to haemoglobinopathies); but the experience of workers in such positions requires us to be cautious about this as the dominant strategy for providing sensitive services.

Many such workers felt marginalised and isolated; perversely some experienced open hostility from white colleagues and users. Significantly, many felt that fighting their corner too vigorously tarnished their reputations and damaged career prospects. Nor did workers always enjoy support from managers or management committees, both predominantly white. This, too, is not uncommon in other fields and there is a clear responsibility on employing agencies to ensure adequate support and redress mechanisms for such workers.

The forgotten groups

Much research as well as action on minority ethnic communities is heavily skewed in favour of the numerically large and geographically concentrated communities. Most texts or research papers in this area focus on the Asian or African Caribbean populations. Our study confirms this concentration. The majority of initiatives were of or for Asian groups, followed by the African Caribbean population. Indeed, even the African Caribbean population felt relatively underserved in this regard, especially when it came to social groups. Particularly poorly served were the smaller minority ethnic communities, the refugee groups and the numerically large but geographically dispersed groups.

We identified very few initiatives focusing on or by minority ethnic communities other than Asians and African Caribbeans. A small number of Jewish deaf organisations were identified; more positively, these were relatively well established and well resourced. The activity focusing on refugees was largely concentrated in London. We are not aware of any service focusing on or an initiative by the Chinese community in this area. The dearth of large-scale community-based provision, or any associated research literature, for the Chinese population is noted by Pui-Ling Li

(1992). The specialist centres offering a range of services are located in London, Manchester and Liverpool and may well be the major sites of support for many in the Chinese community, both in the locality and further afield. The need to provide for the smaller and/or dispersed minority ethnic communities continues to be disregarded in the field of deafness, as in other fields.

There must be an unmet need for support among deaf people from these many and varied communities, justified by the fact that they concern small numbers or the perception that 'they look after their own' (see Walker and Ahmad, 1994; Atkin and Rollings, 1996). Both service providers and the wider deaf community must take action to end this marginalisation.

In terms of deaf people themselves, the focus of provision seemed to be on sign language users (Deaf people) and less on hard of hearing or deafened people. We came across only one example of specialist provision for hard of hearing Asian people and one in lip-reading classes. The national organisation specifically for hard of hearing people, Hearing Concern, had only just begun to address the issue by planning to translate information. This picture reflects the pattern in the Deaf world generally as hard of hearing and deafened people usually do not identify with the Deaf community and specialist provision. We found no initiatives which focused on deaf-blind people or deaf people with other disabilities from minority ethnic communities.

Identity and organisation

An important aspect of our work is that much of the Deaf-led activity so strongly revolves around ethnicity, culture and religion, in some ways representing a quest for a rediscovery of forms of identity which are crucial to people's lives, as discussed in Chapter 5. These forms of identity were often denied to deaf people for a variety of reasons. First, education in schools (including schools for deaf children) has little focus on minority religions, languages and cultures, something pointed out by many young people, their parents and teachers. The Eurocentricity of educational provision was resented by many and is powerfully illustrated in the words of the mother who remarked: "I send my child to school and he comes back an Englishman". Second, Deaf culture remains predominantly white and Christian. Although religious and cultural diversity in Deaf culture is beginning to be recognised, Deaf culture is not yet able to fully accommodate or service this diversity. Third, parents and families have often not been able to communicate easily with their deaf children and hence Deaf adults have had less exposure to their own ethnic culture than would be usual for a hearing person. Many of these issues are addressed in Chamba et al (1998).

However, these developments must not be seen only in negative or compensatory terms; rediscovery and reaffirmation of different forms of identity is not unique to minority ethnic Deaf people. Identity is a potent means of social organisation and of giving meaning to personal and group beliefs, aspirations and behaviour (see Rex, 1991; Joly, 1987; and on religious mobilisation, Samad, 1992). It is not surprising that Deaf people should also organise around such symbols.

That personal identities are negotiated, flexible and situational is also evident in the initiatives discussed here. Social and cultural activity was organised on a variety of grounds: gender, with both young and older people; religion; ethnicity, broadly defined in terms of say 'Asian', though local residence patterns often meant that most users had a more narrowly shared cultural, linguistic and religious background; and Deaf identity. The organisation at these different levels clearly had both advantages and disadvantages. For example, the young Deaf women, who were joined by older hearing women, while resenting the fact that much of what was discussed around deafness was already known to them, were appreciative of the fact that being with older women allowed them to know what would be expected of them as they grew older. For the younger Deaf women, these older women were a major source of cultural knowledge and behavioural norms (see Ahmad, 1996, for broader discussion). Yet in other cases, groups emphasised the shared nature of deafness as being their primary identifier; ethnicity, religion and other cultural identities were secondary and their assertion even considered to be divisive (see Vernon, 1996, for a view on ethnicity and disability). The negotiated nature of identity is discussed by Drury (1991), Modood et al (1994) and Ahmad (1996); and in relation to deafness by Chamba et al (1998).

Empowerment and professionalisation

One strong feature of deafness in recent years is the emergence of Deaf professionals and the proliferation of educational and vocational courses aimed at Deaf people. This was also an issue addressed in some of the initiatives and the importance of role models was emphasised by many. In particular, the relative shortage of African Caribbean role models was noted by both African Caribbean and other respondents, as was their more limited mobilisation compared to Asian Deaf people. Through the fieldwork and personal contacts, we have noted an increase in minority ethnic Deaf professionals in recent years, most themselves working with Deaf people.

The increased self-organisation and lobbying, and greater formal recognition of diversity among deaf/Deaf people should improve training and education opportunities for minority ethnic deaf people in years to come.

The impact of organisation around social and cultural issues may also have positive outcomes in terms of personal development. First, such groups provided opportunities for networking and discovering positive role models, both deaf and hearing. The importance of role models is well recognised in literature on educational achievement and ethnicity (Cashmore and Troyna, 1990). Secondly, they offered access to information and resources. This was important both to families of deaf people who, according to some respondents, often had low expectations for their deaf family members, and to deaf people themselves. Access to information remains a problem for large sections of the minority ethnic population (see Atkin and Rollings, 1993), but for deaf people this is potentially an even bigger problem. Thirdly, a positive identity, which many seemed to be acquiring through their involvement in social activities, is in itself an important element of self-development. Finally, the groups offered an important source of social support, which many felt was absent from the white Deaf culture. As we have noted, although white Deaf culture is increasingly acknowledging diversity among deaf people, there is much room for progress.

Language, communication and family relationships

We explored a number of debates around communication between deaf people and their families in Chapter 6. That both deaf people and their families take the issue of communication seriously is clear from the evidence. The lack of a common language in the family which could allow full participation by the deaf child in family life was recognised by all – deaf young people, families and professionals – as a major problem (as it is with white deaf children). Language choice between BSL, English and other home languages was complex and affected by a range of factors. These included personal knowledge and preferences on the part of parents, professional attitudes, available help and the degree of deafness. Some shift in professional perspectives was noted by parents; whereas once communication in the home language was seen as too confusing for the deaf child, it was now often encouraged. However, speech therapy support remained largely confined to the English language both for young children and cochlear implant patients, although some rare attempts to offer speech therapy in other languages were noted. Limited support for lip-reading in languages other than English was also noted.

Young Deaf people regretted that lack of access to a home language had often made their own cultures and religions inaccessible, and parents worried about ensuring that their children learned about community and religious values. Considering the importance of a shared language in fostering family and community ties, the level of concern both from parents and deaf people is understandable. The older children's reliance on BSL and, where they have speech, on English, often excludes them from routine family life and this may particularly affect the mother's relationship with the child (Mahon et al, 1995). Among Asian, Chinese and many other minority ethnic groups, English is not universally used and women have lower rates of fluency and literacy in English than men (HEA, 1994; Modood et al, 1997).

Parents were not complacent about communication difficulties, however. We have described a range of initiatives around learning BSL and/or sign-supported English. The initiatives varied in focus and ethos: some were predominantly self-help groups with some autonomy, others represented more formal efforts at teaching sign language. Most tended to be flexible: in addition to learning signing, parents could obtain information and seek advice and practical help, and learn from other parents. Some also offered translated written notes or videos of signs practised during the class, which parents could then practise with other family members. In addition to learning signing, benefits of attending included increased confidence, social support, information and access to networks. Literature shows that minority ethnic communities tend to be less well informed about welfare rights and the role of institutions and professionals (Cameron et al, 1989; Ahmad and Walker, 1997). Practical help from and reliance on professionals and voluntary workers for information emerge as particularly valued aspects of user contact with services (Chapters 6 and 7). Surprisingly, most classes were taught by hearing teachers of BSL, something which is not reflected in national BSL teacher training policy.

That sign language groups consisted mainly of mothers, with few fathers attending, may reflect the gendered nature of caring and the greater role played by mothers with younger children. Evidence suggests that, compared to fathers, mothers tend to be more knowledgeable about their child's condition and needs (Ahmad and Atkin, 1996a). However, in the few initiatives which provided written materials for use at home, mothers often worked with fathers and siblings in practising the signs between themselves and with the deaf child. Physical access to groups was an important factor for mothers as was the availability of transport.

Overcoming language barriers

Ascribing issues of access to and equity in services to language barriers is a classic form of reductionism in British social policy (Pearson, 1986; Ahmad,

1989). This having been said, the hardship experienced by users whose preferred language is different from that used by the majority of professionals is very real and a number of problems were discussed by respondents. One was that of using family members as interpreters, or using interpreters from other services in an area where they had insufficient knowledge of service context or terminology and little rapport with other professionals. Using family members as interpreters is regarded as wholly unsatisfactory, although large numbers of people have no option but to rely on family and friends (Richter et al, 1979; Ahmad and Walker, 1997). Problems include poor knowledge of terminology, issues around confidentiality, rapport with practitioners and, in the case of children, a reversal of the conventional child–parent relationship. In relation to primary care, Ahmad et al (1989) argue that due to communication problems experienced in gaining access to general practice, many women may be foregoing treatment or resorting to treatment from male doctors, against their ideal preference, because of the severe shortage of female doctors who speak Asian languages. This is a particular problem for mothers, who are likely to carry a greater share of care for a deaf child. They may have to cope with fewer resources, including inadequate information, while having to go through a larger number of 'gate-keepers', including interpreters. Lay interpreting in sign language is a particular issue where serious attempts are being made to separate the interpreting and advocacy roles (see Chapter 3). It was encouraging, however, that professionals recognised clear benefits from improved communication (see Chapter 6).

Difficulties in access to information and resources led to a variety of problems: bewilderment, parents not knowing what is expected of them, inadequate information about prognosis, and choices for the future being made in an information vacuum. Although language problems are noted to lead to greater compliance with professional advice (Watson, 1984; Bhopal, 1986; Bhopal and Samim, 1988), this represents professional control through enforced ignorance and is thus unacceptable. Chamba et al (1998) note that parents of deaf children valued information on a wide range of issues concerning their children. This information was not always sought during the diagnostic consultation, however, and parents were critical of the lack of opportunity to seek information from consultants. Their main source of information were the peripatetic teachers of deaf children, whose support was much valued. Issues of access to information are also explored by Atkin et al (1997) in relation to Asian and African Caribbean parents' experiences of caring for a child with sickle cell disorder or thalassaemia major.

Sign language interpreting

It was generally acknowledged that there were insufficient minority ethnic sign language interpreters, and in particular an acute shortage of Asian interpreters. The need will only be met by improved recruitment of people from the relevant ethnic groups. The advantages of having more Asian and other minority ethnic interpreters are several and varied. There is a dearth of interpreters who can interpret between BSL and languages other than English and filling this gap will help improve communication. Secondly, white interpreters often do not have the requisite knowledge of minority ethnic customs, rituals, foods, festivals (see Chapters 5 and 6). Many also pointed out the racism of sign language, although many of the openly offensive signs are being changed. Thirdly, some felt that even where minority ethnic interpreters and deaf people did not share a common culture or language, they had shared experiences of being in a dominant white culture, which improved rapport and encouraged trust. However, the lack of access to the limited training opportunities and the failure to attract minority ethnic trainee interpreters remains a problem to be urgently addressed.

Cultural sensitivity

Cultural sensitivity in service delivery is sometimes regarded as being in opposition to an anti-racist approach to providing services – an issue explored by Stubbs (1993). We would argue that a recognition of both the racialised nature of society and racism experienced by minority ethnic people, and of cultural and religious traditions, is important in providing appropriate services. The latter require both a sensitivity to people's cultures and to the realities of racism. Although we note a lack of progress in the voluntary sector and instances of racism in Deaf centres, there was sensitivity on the part of many service providers that Western ideas about deafness cannot be imposed on minority ethnic deaf people or their families. This is interesting in that ethnic diversity or the legitimacy of separate organisation by minority ethnic disabled people is not readily recognised by many in the disability movement (see Begum et al, 1994, for a critique). Fears are expressed about the divisive nature of such separate organisation (Oliver, 1995;Vernon, 1996), an argument reminiscent of the anti-racist position in relation to struggles on cultural or religious grounds (Sivanandan, 1990).

The recognition of the need to provide appropriate services includes consideration of time and venue, gender (separate groups may be appropriate at times), convenience, and availability of transport. However, as we discuss below, funding mechanisms often create tensions between user defined needs and the remit of specific initiatives. The official recognition of need is reflected in many initiatives having been started by committed professionals, many of them white. This, however, does not always constitute a culture change on the part of the organisation; the problems of the 'specialist worker' approach to ethnic sensitivity are addressed in Chapters 4 and 8.

It is interesting to note that the stereotypes of Asian women as passive and uncritical continue. Although there is some evidence of their greater likelihood of uncritical acceptance of professional advice, there is abundant proof of their initiative and energy in the range of social and cultural projects which are largely driven by Asian women as discussed in Chapter 5. Indeed, this is seen as a positive feature of social organisation of Asian Deaf people by the African Caribbean Deaf people who wish to emulate the former's success.

The most important aspect of a sensitive service seemed to be the flexibility to respond to user needs. Users found it difficult to compartmentalise their needs and workers were not always able to fit user demands into their remit, as discussed in Chapter 7. Minority ethnic workers in statutory organisations expressed concerns about becoming 'interpreters' for white professionals. Although they expressed a commitment to improving services they felt it inappropriate to have to be reduced to the role of interpreter, for which they had no training, and which allowed them less time for the tasks consistent with their job descriptions. We have discussed the problems of using untrained interpreters in Chapters 5 and 7. The 'dumping' of all 'specialist' cases to minority ethnic staff also acts as an excuse for continued organisational incompetence in dealing with minority ethnic clients, as discussed above (and in Chapter 5). Voluntary and specialist organisations have often been at the forefront of sensitive service delivery.

Voluntary and specialist organisations

We witnessed a general feeling of non-recognition of difference on part of deaf voluntary organisations, with very few of the large deaf organisations undertaking any major or sustained initiative to reach out to minority ethnic users or members. The few positive responses included the recent work by the NDCS involving minority ethnic parents, and by the BDA and RNID. Some other organisations have done work focusing on minority ethnic communities, but, on the whole, this remains marginal to the main interests of deaf voluntary organisations which revolve around serving and representing white deaf people. The situation is not dissimilar to what Rooney and McKain (1990) describe in relation to voluntary services with a health focus or to what Cochrane and Sashidharan (1996) note in relation to voluntary organisations around alcohol abuse. Rooney and McKain reported little focus on minority ethnic communities as users, little involvement from them on management committees and few opportunities as volunteers. Cochrane and Sashidharan (1996) note that, compared to white people, a greater proportion of Asians with alcohol-related problems were resorting to medical solutions and that their use of relatively inaccessible voluntary sector provision was negligible.

Marginalisation in Deaf centres was also noted by both Asian and African Caribbean users and minority ethnic workers. Apart from instances of blatant racism, they experienced resentment towards targeted provision, interpreted as preferential treatment and a diversion of resources from white to minority ethnic deaf people. Some respondents perceived similar marginalisation to take place in the Deaf media's treatment of minority ethnic deaf people. Concerns about recognising ethnic diversity and its relationship with differential individual and group experiences have been explored in other chapters in this report, and are the subject of recent debates in the disability movement (for example, Begum et al, 1994).

Funding and its implications

Funding sources and constraints had important implications for service development, user involvement and systems of accountability. First, the short-term nature of much funding for 'special initiatives' made longer-term planning difficult. There was pressure on workers to show that the work was worthy of continued support. This could only be achieved by creating a balance between project work, monitoring and evaluation to support claims for continued support and efforts to gain new funding. Effort was often diverted from the work itself and to presentation and evaluation of work for the benefit of funders. Secondly, the limited knowledge of funding sources and underdeveloped skills in securing funding in the voluntary sector were difficult problems to overcome – a concern noted in relation to minority ethnic voluntary sector generally, (Atkin, 1996). This may also mean that Deaf workers have to look to hearing allies for support in securing funding.

Thirdly, the restrictions on how the funding could be spent created tensions, with workers having to accommodate user-defined needs into funder-defined remits. Where such restrictions were not imposed, the work was usually more flexible and there was greater user involvement in decision making. Attempts were made by workers, often themselves Deaf, to develop packages of funding to support different aspects of their work. This both offered greater flexibility within the package and added appreciably to the burdens carried by workers to maintain a constant flow of funding from various sources.

The impact of funding on the development of services and the relationship with users is discussed by Watters (1996) in relation to voluntary and 'specialist' mental health provision aimed at Asian people. We find remarkably similar problems to those described by Watters, who also notes that the purchaser–provider split in health and social services creates further difficulties for such initiatives (see also Jeyasingham, 1992). One such difficulty is that the flexible nature of many such initiatives – where the work may include a combination of 'need assessment', advocacy and campaigning, and service provision – is compromised, in that the need assessment and advocacy roles may be regarded as resting with the 'purchaser' rather than the voluntary sector 'provider'.

Whereas difference in need and perspectives was recognised for the Asian community, African Caribbean respondents felt that they were regarded as having no 'specific cultural needs'. This was confirmed by professionals claiming that African Caribbean deaf people's needs could easily be accommodated in mainstream services. The view highlights both the difficulty of having demands recognised as legitimate on part of the African Caribbean deaf people, and the strength of the stereotype that African Caribbean culture is no more than an impoverished version of white culture (for a detailed discussion, see Lawrence in CCCS, 1982).

Interagency working

Finally, we have discussed some examples of useful cross-agency work. An important aspect of service delivery valued by users and their families is a well coordinated service with a 'single door' or 'key worker' approach (Glendinning, 1985). In Chamba et al's (1998) study of Asian parents with deaf children, the key worker role, often played by the peripatetic teacher, was highly valued. Similarly valued is the coordinating role played by haemoglobinopathy counsellors in relation to sickle cell disorder and thalassaemia (Atkin et al, 1997). However, the boundaries across health, social services, education and other providers sometimes created problems – an issue of increasing importance also in the work of the voluntary sector, as we have noted.

Conclusion

That minority ethnic deaf people have an increasing profile is not in doubt. There is a greater recognition of their needs among a range of service providers and they have an increasing involvement in Deaf politics. It is also clear from our work that the range of developments paint a mixed picture; alongside some positive changes, much of the activity emulates the culture of 'special needs' provision once witnessed in social work and health more generally. This has two major disadvantages. Firstly, it marginalises minority ethnic deaf people's needs as well as the status of 'specialist workers' within predominantly white organisations. Secondly, the needs of certain groups, such as the African Caribbean, may not be recognised as they are not deemed sufficiently 'culturally different' from the white population.

Whereas ethnic diversity among deaf people is increasingly being recognised it does not always translate into action to respect diversity or to respond to culturally different requirements. This comes out strongly in minority ethnic Deaf people's critiques of the deaf organisations, and is implicit in the rise of self-organisation around ethnic and religious identity. However, barriers to education, training and employment remain.

More difficult to follow is the progress of hard of hearing, deafened and deaf-blind people from minority ethnic communities - they seem to be hidden from any of the initiatives considered in this book. This may not be due to a lack of needs but rather a reflection of inaccessible and inappropriate services, suggesting a similar pattern to that among white people from these groups. This, and the difficulty in contacting deaf people from smaller minority ethnic communities, are the two noticeable absences from the initiatives we have identified.

The self-organisation is coupled with an attempt by parents and families of deaf people to learn more about deafness and sign language. The strength of this self-organisation indicates the determination of minority ethnic deaf people to play a role in defining themselves and their needs, not just as deaf people but as people who hold dearly their cultural, religious and gender identities.

References

Afshar, H. (1994) 'Muslim women in West Yorkshire: growing up with real and imaginary values amidst conflicting views of self and society', in H. Afshar and M. Maynards (eds) *The dynamics of 'race' and gender: Some feminist interventions*, London: Taylor and Francis.

Ahmad, W.I.U. (1989) 'Policies, pills and political will: critique of policies to improve the health of ethnic minorities', *Lancet* I, pp 148-50.

Ahmad, W.I.U. (1993) *'Race' and health in contemporary Britain*, Buckingham: Open University Press.

Ahmad, W.I.U. (1994) 'Reflections on the consanguinity and birth outcome debate', *Journal of Public Health Medicine*, vol 16, no 4, pp 423-8.

Ahmad, W.I.U. (1996) 'Family obligations and social change in Asian communities: implications for community care', in W.I.U. Ahmad and K. Atkin (eds) *'Race' and community care*, Buckingham: Open University Press.

Ahmad, W.I.U. (in press) 'Ethnic statistics: better than nothing or worse than nothing?', in D. Dorling and S. Simpson (eds) *Statistics and society*, London: Arnold.

Ahmad, W.I.U. and Atkin, K. (1996a) 'Ethnicity and caring for a disabled child: the case of children with sickle cell or thalassaemia', *British Journal of Social Work*, vol 26, pp 755–75.

Ahmad, W.I.U. and Atkin, K. (1996b) *'Race' and community care*, Buckingham: Open University Press.

Ahmad, W.I.U. and Husband, C. (1993) 'Religious identity, citizenship and welfare: the case of Muslims in Britain', *American Journal of Islamic Social Science*, vol 10, no 2, pp 217-33.

Ahmad, W.I.U. and Walker, R. (1997) 'Asian older people: housing, health and access to services', *Ageing and Society*, vol 17, pp 141-65.

Ahmad, W.I.U., Atkin, K. and Chamba, R. (forthcoming) '"Causing havoc among their children": professional and parental perspectives on consanguinity and childhood disability"', *Sociology of Health and Illness*.

Ahmad, W.I.U., Kernohan, E.E.M. and Baker, M.R. (1989) 'Patients' choice of general practitioner: influence of patients' fluency in English and the ethnicity and sex of the doctor', *Journal of the Royal College of General Practitioners*, vol 39, pp 153-5.

Ahmed, A.S. (1988) *Discovering Islam: Making sense of Muslim history and society*, London: Routledge.

Ahmed, R. (ed) (1991) *We sinful women: Contemporary Urdu feminist poetry*, London: Women's Press.

Akhtar, S. (1989) *Be careful with Mohammad*, London: Grey Seal.

Alladin, W. (1992) 'Clinical psychology provision: models, policies and prospects', in W.I.U. Ahmad (ed) *The politics of 'race' and health*, Bradford: Race Relations Unit, University of Bradford.

Anthias, F. (1992) *Ethnicity, class, gender and migration: Greek Cypriots in Britain*, Aldershot: Avebury.

Anthias, F. and Yuval-Davis, F. (1993) *Racialized boundaries*, London: Routledge.

Anwar, M. (1977) *The myth of return: Pakistanis in Britain*, London: Heinemann.

Atkin, K. (1996) 'An opportunity for change: voluntary sector provision in a mixed economy of care', in W.I.U. Ahmad and K. Atkin (eds) *'Race' and community care*, Buckingham: Open University Press.

Atkin, K. and Rollings, J. (1993) *Community care in a multi-racial society*, London: HMSO.

Atkin, K. and Rollings, J. (1996) 'They look after their own', in W.I.U. Ahmad and K. Atkin (eds) *'Race' and community care*, Buckingham: Open University Press.

Atkin, K., Ahmad, W.I.U. and Anionwu, E. (1997) *Evaluation of services for children with sickle cell disorders or thalassaemia major*, final report to NHS Research and Development Initiative on Physical and Complex Disability, Bradford: ESPR.

Badat, H. and Whall-Roberts, D. (1994) *Bridging the gap: Creating services for deaf people from ethnic minority communities*, London: RNID.

Baker, R. (1991) 'Information technology: a breakthrough for deaf people?', in S. Gregory and G.M. Hartley (eds) *Constructing deafness*, London: Pinter.

BDA (British Deaf Association) (1994) *BDA News*, February.

Beaudry, J. and Hetu, R. (1991) 'Measurement of attitudes of those with impaired hearing towards the hearing impaired', *Journal of Speech, Language Pathology and Audiology*, vol 2, no 14, pp 23-32.

Becker, G. (1980) *Growing old in silence*, Berkeley: University of California Press.

Begum, N. (1992) 'Doubly disabled', *Community Care*, September, 934, pp iii-iv.

Begum, N. (1994) 'Mirror, mirror on the wall', in N. Begum, M. Hill and A. Stevens, *Reflections: The views of black disabled people on their lives and community care*, London: CCETSW.

Begum, N., Hill, M. and Vernon, A. (1994) *Reflections: The views of black disabled people on their lives and community care*, London: CCETSW.

Bellman, S. and Marcuson, M. (1991) 'A new toy test to investigate the hearing status of young children who have English as a second language', *British Journal of Audiology*, vol 25, pp 317-22.

Bhachu, P. (1988) '*Apni marzi kardi*: home and work. Sikh women in Britain', in S. Westwood and P. Bhachu (eds) *Enterprising women: Ethnicity, economy and gender relations*, London: Routledge.

Bhopal, R. (1986) 'Asians' knowledge and behaviour on preventive health issues', *Community Medicine*, vol 8, pp 315-21.

Bhopal, R. (1992) 'Future research on health of ethnic minorities', in W.I.U. Ahmad (ed) *The politics of 'race' and health*, Bradford: Race Relations Unit, Bradford University.

Bhopal, R. and Samim, A.K. (1988) 'Immunization uptake of Glasgow Asian children: paradoxical benefit of communication barriers', *Community Medicine*, vol 10, pp 215-20.

Blakemore, K. and Boneham, M. (1994) *Age, race and ethnicity*, Buckingham: Open University Press.

Brennan, M., Colville, M. and Lawson, L. (1980) *Words in hand: A structural analysis of the signs in British Sign Language*, Edinburgh: Moray House.

Bryan, B., Dadzie, S. and Scafe, S. (1985) *The heart of the race: Black women's lives in Britain*, London: Virago.

Burghart, R. (1987) *Hinduism in Great Britain*, London: Tavistock.

Butt, J. and Mirza, K. (1996) *Social care and black communities*, London: HMSO.

Cameron, E., Badger, F., Evens, H. and Atkins, K. (1989) 'Black old women, disability and health care', in M. Jeffreys (ed) *Growing old in the twentieth century*, London: Routledge.

Cashmore, E. (ed) (1988) *Dictionary of race and ethnic relations*, London: Routledge.

Cashmore, E. and Troyna, B. (1990) *Introduction to race relations*, London: Falmer.

CCCS (Centre for Contemporary Cultural Studies) (1982) *The empire strikes back*, London: Hutchinson.

Chamba, R., Ahmad, W.I.U. and Jones, L. (1998) *Improving services for Asian Deaf children*, Bradford: ESPR.

Chamba, R., Ahmad, W.I.U., Darr, A. and Jones, L. (in press) 'Education of Asian deaf children', in S. Gregory, P. Knight, W. McCrackon, S. Powers and L. Watson, L. (eds) *Education of deaf children*, London: David Fulton Publishing.

Christensen, K. and Delgado, G. (1993) *Multicultural issues in deafness*, White Plains, NY: Longman.

Cochrane, R. and Sashidharan, S. (1996) 'Mental health and ethnic minorities: review of literature and implications for services', in W.I.U. Ahmad, T. Sheldon and O. Stuart (eds) *Ethnicity and health: Reviews of literature and guidance for purchasers in the areas of cardiovascular disease, mental health and haemoglobinopathies*, York: NHS Centre for Reviews and Dissemination.

Conrad, R. (1979) *The deaf schoolchild*, London: Harper & Row.

Cooper J. (1995) *Health needs assessment for children with hearing impairment*, unpublished draft report, Bradford Health Authority.

Corker, M. (1994) *Counselling – the deaf challenge*, London: Jessica Kingsley.

Coupar, K. (1996) *Insight: The touch and go final report*, Durham CACDP.

Craig, G. and Rai, D.K. (1996) 'Social security, community care – and 'race': the marginal dimensions', in W.I.U. Ahmad and K. Atkin (eds) *'Race' and community care*, Buckingham: Open University Press.

Crawford, R. (1977) 'You are dangerous to your health: the ideology and politics of victim blaming', *International Journal of Health Services*, vol 7, no 4, pp 663-80.

CSO (Central Statistical Office) (1996) *Social focus on ethnic minorities*, London: HMSO.

Darr, A., Jones, L., Ahmad, W.I.U. and Nisar, G. (1997) *A directory of initiatives on ethnicity and deafness*, SPRU, York University/ESPR, Bradford University.

Davies, A. (1987) 'Epidemiology of hearing disorders', in D. Stephens (ed) *Audiology*, London: Butterworth.

Drury, B. (1991) 'Sikh girls and the maintenance of an ethnic culture', *New Community*, vol 17, no 3, pp 387-99.

Ellis, B. (1994) *Disabled women's report*, London: Greater London Association of Disabled People.

Finkelstein, V. (1991) 'We are not disabled you are', in S. Gregory and G. M. Hartley (eds) *Constructing deafness*, London: Pinter.

Fortnum, H.M., Davis, A.C., Butler, A. and Stevens, J. (1996) *Health service implications of changes in aetiology and referral patterns of hearing impaired children in Trent 1985 – 1993*, Sheffield: Trent Health.

Gerrish, K., Husband, C. and Mackenzie, J. (1996) *Nursing for a multi-ethnic society*, Buckingham: Open University Press.

Gilroy, P. (1990) 'The end of anti-racism', in W. Ball and J. Solomos (eds) *'Race' and local politics*, Basingstoke: Macmillan.

Glendinning, C. (1985) *A single door*, London: George Allen and Unwin.

Goel, K., Sweet, E.M., Campbell, S. et al (1981) 'Reduced prevalence of rickets in Asian children in Glasgow', *Lancet* I, pp 945-6.

Grant, B. (1987) *The quiet ear: Deafness in literature*, East Lothian: The Pentland Press.

Grant, B. (1990) *A history of the BDA*, East Lothian: The Pentland Press.

Gregory, S. and Hartley, G.M. (1991) *Constructing deafness*, London: Pinter.

Gregory, S., Bishop, J. and Sheldon, L. (1995) *Deaf young people and their families*, Cambridge: Cambridge University Press.

Groce, N. (1985) *Everyone there spoke sign language*, Cambridge, MA: Harvard University Press.

Harris, J. (1995) *The cultural meaning of deafness*, Aldershot: Avebury.

Harrison, M. (1993) 'The black voluntary housing movement: pioneering pluralistic social policy in a difficult climate', *Critical Social Policy*, vol 39, pp 21-35.

HEA (Health Education Authority) (1994) *Black and minority ethnic groups in England*, London: HEA.

Hevey, D. (1993) *The creatures that time forgot*, London: Routledge.

Higgins, P. (1988) *Outsiders in a hearing world*, Beverly Hills.

Hill, M. (1994) '"They are not our brothers": the disability movement and the black disability movement', in N. Begum, M. Hill and A. Stevens (eds) *Reflections:The views of black disabled people on their lives and community care*, London: CCETSW.

Hoffmeister, R. (1996) 'Crosscultural misinformation: what does special education say about deaf people', *Disability and Society*, vol 11, no 2, pp 171-89.

Holcombe, M. and Wood, S. (1989) *Deaf women:A parade through the decades*, Berkeley CA: Dawn Sign Press.

Husband, C. (1994) *'Race' and nation:The British experience*, Perth, Australia: Paradigm Books.

Imtiaz, S. and Johnson, M. (1993) *Heath care provision and the Kashmiri population of Peterborough*, Peterborough Race Equality Council.

Jackson, P. (1990) *Britain's deaf heritage*, Edinburgh: Pentland Press.

Jeyasingham, M. (1992) 'Acting for health: ethnic minorities and the community health movement', in W.I.U.Ahmad (ed) *The politics of 'race' and health*, Bradford: Race Relations Unit, University of Bradford.

Johnson, M.R.D. (1996) *Ethnic minorities, health and communication*, Warwick University: Centre for Research in Ethnic Relations.

Joly, D. (1987) 'Associations amongst Pakistani population in Britain', in J. Rex and D. Joly with C. Wilpert (eds) *Immigrant associations in Europe*, Aldershot: Gower.

Jones, L. (1993) *Education and deaf and hard of hearing adults*, Leicester: National Institute of Adult and Continuing Education.

Jones, L. (1987) *Words apart: Losing your hearing as an adult*, London:Tavistock.

Jones, L. and Pullen, G. (1989) 'Inside we are all equal: a European social policy survey of people who are deaf', in L. Barton (ed) *Disability and dependency*, London: Falmer Press.

Jones, L. and Pullen, G. (1992) 'Cultural differences: deaf and hearing researchers working together', *Disability Handicap and Society*, vol 7, no 2, pp 189-96.

Kohli, K. (1990) *A survey into the needs of Asian people with a hearing impairment and their carers in Leicester*, Leicester: Leicester Centre for the Deaf.

Kyle, J. (1991) 'Some aspects of sign language/English interpreting', *Deafness*, vol 1, no 5.

Kyle, J. and Woll, B. (1985) *Sign language: The study of deaf people and their language*, Cambridge: Cambridge University Press.

Ladd, P. (1990) 'Making plans for Nigel: the erosion of identity by main streaming', in G. Taylor and J. Bishop (eds) *Being deaf: The experience of deafness*, London: Pinter.

Ladd, P. (1991) 'The modern deaf community', in S. Gregory and G.M. Hartley (eds) *Constructing deafness*, London: Pinter.

Lane, H. (1984) *When the mind hears: A history of the Deaf*, New York: Random House.

Lane, H. (1993) *The mask of benevolence: Disabling the Deaf community*, New York: Vintage Books.

Lane, H. (1995) 'Constructions of deafness', *Disability and Society*, vol 10, no 2, pp 171-89.

Lane, H. and Grodin, M. (1997) 'Ethical issues in cochlear implants surgery', *Kennedy Institute of Ethics Journal*, vol 7, no 3, pp 231-51.

Lane, H., Hoffmeister R. and Bahan, B. (1996) *A journey into the deaf-world*, San Diego CA: Dawn Sign Press.

Leicester Black Mental Health Group (1988) *Sadness in my heart*, Leicester: Department of Sociology.

Lewis, P. (1994) *Islamic Britain*, London: I.B. Taurus.

Li, Pui-Ling (1992) 'Health needs of the Chinese population', in W.I.U. Ahmad (ed) *The politics of 'race' and health*, Bradford: Race Relations Unit, Bradford University.

Lumb, K.M. (1981) 'Prevalence of hearing loss in children of Asian origin', *Proceedings of the Scientific Meeting of the British Association of Audiological Physicians and Community Paediatric Group*, pp 60-5.

Lynas, W. and Turner, S. (1995) *Young children with sensori-neural hearing loss from ethnic minority families: Provision by educational services in England*, Centre for Audiology, Education of the Deaf and Speech Pathology, University of Manchester.

Mahon, M., Wells, B. and Tarplee, C. (1995) *Conversational strategies of deaf children and their families where English is the second language*, Report to the ESRC.

McNaught, A. (1987) *Health action and ethnic minorities*, London: National Community Health Resource.

Mercer, K. (1986) 'Racism and transcultural psychiatry', in P. Miller and N. Rose (eds) *The Power of psychiatry*, Cambridge: Polity Press.

Modood, T. (1988) '"Black", racial equality and Asian identity', *New Community*, vol 14, no 3, pp 397-404.

Modood, T., Beishon, S. and Virdee, S. (1994) *Changing ethnic identities*, London: Policy Studies Institute.

Modood, T., Berthoud, R., Lakey, J., Nazroo, J., Smith, P., Virdee, S. and Beishon, S. (1997) *Ethnic minorities in Britain: Diversity and disadvantage*, London: Policy Studies Institute.

Myklebust, H.R. (1960) *The psychology of deafness*, New York and London: Grune and Stratton.

Naeem, Z. and Newton, V. (1996) 'The prevalence of sensori-neural hearing loss in Asian children', *British Journal of Audiology*, vol 30, no 5, pp 332-40.

Noble, W. (1991) 'Assessment of impaired hearing', in S. Gregory and G.M. Hartley (eds) *Constructing deafness*, London: Pinter Publishers.

Nuru, N. (1993) 'Multi-cultural aspects of deafness', in D. Battle (ed) *Communication disorders in multi-cultural populations*, Stoneham, MA: Andover Medical Publishers.

Odegaard, O. (1932) cited in R. Littlewood and M. Lipsedge (1989) *Aliens and alienists: Ethnic minorities and psychiatry*, London: Unwin Hyman.

OPCS (Office of Population Censuses and Statistics) (1985) *The prevalence of disability among adults*, London: HMSO.

Oliver, M. (1995) 'Review of *Reflections*', *Disability and Society*, vol 10, pp 369-71.

Oliver, M (1996) *Understanding disability from theory to practice,* Basingstoke: Macmillan.

Open University (1991; 1995) *Issues in deafness* (various course units), Buckingham: Open University Press.

Padden, C. and Humphries, T. (1988) *Deaf in America – Voices from a culture,* Cambridge, MA: Harvard University Press.

Patel, N. (1993) 'Health margins: black elders' care', in W.I.U. Ahmad (ed) *'Race' and health in contemporary Britain,* Buckingham: Open University Press.

Pearson, M. (1986) 'Racist notions of ethnicity and culture in health education', in S. Rodmell and A. Watt (eds) *The politics of health promotion,* London: Tavistock.

Preston, P. (1995) *Mother father deaf; Living between sound and silence,* Cambridge, MA: Harvard University Press.

Rex, J. (1991) *Ethnic identity and ethnic mobilisation in Britain,* Warwick: Centre for Research in Ethnic Relations.

Richter, R., Daly, S. and Clarke, J. (1979) 'Overcoming language difficulties with migrant patients', *Medical Journal of Australia,* vol 1, pp 275-6.

Rocheron, Y. (1988) 'The Asian Mother and Baby Campaign: the construction of ethnic minority health needs', *Critical Social Policy,* vol 22, pp 4-23.

Rooney, B. and McKain, J. (1990) *Voluntary health organisations and the black community in Liverpool,* Liverpool: Sociology Department, University of Liverpool.

Sacks, O. (1989) *Seeing voices,* London: Picador.

Saggar-Malik, S. (1984) 'Unequal access to health care', in G. Somerville (ed) *Community development and health: Addressing the confusions,* London: King's Fund.

Samad, Y. (1992) 'Book burning and race relations: political mobilisation of Bradford Muslims', *New Community,* vol 18, no 4, pp 507-20.

Schein, J.D. and Delk, M.T. (1974) *The deaf population of the United States,* Silver Spring MD: National Association of the Deaf.

Schuchman, J.S. (1991) 'Hollywood speaks: deafness and the film entertainment industry', in S. Gregory and G.M. Hartley (eds) *Constructing deafness,* London: Pinter.

Scott, R.A. (1981) *The making of blind men*, New Brunswick, NJ: Transaction.

Scully, D. and Bart, P. (1978) 'A funny thing happened to me on the way to the orifice: women in gynaecology textbooks', in J. Ehrenreich (ed) *The cultural crisis of modern medicine*, New York and London: Monthly Review Press.

Shah, R. (1986) *Attitudes, stereotypes and service provision*, Manchester: Community Relations Council.

Sharma, A and Love, D. (1991) A *change in approach: A report on the experience of deaf people from black and ethnic minority communities*, London: The Royal Association in Aid of Deaf People.

Shaw, A. (1988) *A Pakistani community in Britain*, Oxford: Blackwell.

Singh, R. (1992) *Immigrants to citizens: The Sikh community in Bradford*, Bradford: Race Relations Unit, University of Bradford.

Sivanandan, A. (1990) *Communities of resistance: Writings on black struggles for socialism*, London: Verso.

Smaje, C. (1995) *Health, 'race' and ethnicity: Making sense of the evidence*, London: King's Fund Institute.

Speedy, J. (1987) 'Breaking down barriers', *TALK*, no 125.

Stokoe, W.C. (1960) *Sign language structure: Studies in linguistics*, Occasional Paper No 8, University of Buffalo.

Stokoe, W.C. (1972) *Semiotics and human sign language*, New York: New York Humanities.

Stuart, O. (1992) 'Race and disability: just a double discrimination', *Disability and Society*, vol 7, no 2, pp 177-88.

Stuart, O. (1994) 'Journey from the margin: black disabled people and the antiracist debate', in N. Begum, M. Hill and A. Stevens (eds) *Reflections: The views of black disabled people on their lives and community care*, London: CCETSW.

Stuart, O. (1996) '"Yes, we mean black disabled people too": thoughts on community care and disabled people from black and minority ethnic communities', in W.I.U. Ahmad and K. Atkin (eds) *'Race' and community care*, Buckingham: Open University Press.

Stubbs, P. (1993) '"Ethnically sensitive" or "anti-racist": models for health research and service delivery', in W.I.U. Ahmad (ed) *'Race' and health in contemporary Britain*, Buckingham: Open University Press.

Thomas, A.J. and Herbst, K.G. (1980) 'Social and psychological implications of acquired deafness in adults of employment age', *British Journal of Audiology*, vol 14, pp 76-85.

Vanniasegaram, I., Tungland, O.P. and Bellman, S. (1993) 'A 5 year review of children with deafness in a multiethnic community', *Journal of Audiological Medicine*, vol 2, pp 9-19.

Vernon, A. (1996) 'Fighting two different battles: unity is preferable to enmity', *Disability and Society*, vol 11, pp 285-90.

Walker, R. and Ahmad, W.I.U. (1994) 'Windows of opportunity in rotting frames; care providers' perspectives on community care and black communities', *Critical Social Policy*, vol 40, pp 46-69.

Watson, E. (1984) 'Health of infants and use of health services by mothers of different ethnic groups in East London', *Community Medicine*, vol 6, pp 127-35.

Watters, C. (1996) 'Representations and realities: black people, mental health and community care', in W.I.U. Ahmad and K. Atkin (eds) *'Race' and community care*, Buckingham: Open University Press.

Werbner, P. (1991) 'The fiction of unity in ethnic politics – aspects of representation and the state among British Pakistanis', in P. Werbner and M. Anwar (eds) *Black and ethnic leaderships: The cultural dimensions of political action*, London: Routledge.

Westwood, S. and Bhachu, P. (1988) *Enterprising women: Ethnicity, economy and gender relations*, London: Routledge.

Woodward, J. (1982) 'Beliefs about and attitudes towards deaf people and sign language on Providence Island', in J. Woodward (ed) *How you gonna get to heaven if you can't talk with Jesus: On depathologising deafness*, Maryland: T J Publishers.

Woolley, M. (1987) 'Acquired hearing loss, acquired expression', in J.G. Kyle (ed) *Adjustment to acquired hearing loss*, Bristol: Centre for Deaf Studies, University of Bristol, pp 172-3.

Yardley, L. (1997) 'The quest for natural communication: technology, language and deafness', *Health*, vol 1, no 1, pp 37-55.

Young, J. (1990) Preface to P. Jackson, *Britain's deaf heritage*, Edinburgh: Pentland Press.

Appendix:
Project aims and methods

This project developed out of a recognition that little was known about minority ethnic deaf people, yet anecdotal evidence pointed to considerable recent interest in ethnicity and deafness at the level of policy and practice. In particular we had been aware of the emergence of the Asian Deaf parties, and the increasing visibility of Asian and African Caribbean Deaf people in Deaf politics and events. This text is an attempt to chart these developments. The work was funded by the Joseph Rowntree Foundation (JRF) and the researchers were supported by an experienced and resourceful Project Advisory Committee. The research team consisted of one Deaf and three hearing people; between them the researchers had skills in BSL and in relevant Asian languages as well as English.

Project aims

The project aims were to:

- provide an overview of existing initiatives, both in the statutory and voluntary sectors, focusing on deaf people from minority ethnic communities, including children;

- obtain information, through documentation and interviews with project and advisory staff about the ethos, focus, funding arrangements, level of community involvement and mechanisms for user accountability, models of practice and location (geographical as well as institutional and disciplinary);

- provide users' perspectives on a sub-sample of these projects and, on the basis of these accounts and other information, identify examples of service provision which are sensitive and accessible.

In addition we undertook to produce a directory of these projects (Darr et al, 1997).

Methods

The data were collected in four broad stages using a variety of methods.

Stage 1

We started with advice from our Project Advisory Committee. A pre-survey, fact-finding workshop was held in Bradford. The 14 participants consisted of minority ethnic deaf people, parents of deaf children and professionals working in the field. Gohar Nisar, the Deaf consultant to the project, facilitated the workshop. A number of preliminary interviews with relevant people were also conducted to help focus the work and extend our networks.

Stage 2

This stage consisted of a postal survey of statutory and voluntary agencies with which people, deaf and hearing, come into contact. A brief questionnaire was used to collect information on any form of initiative targeted at minority ethnic deaf people. The questionnaire and a covering letter were sent to the following agencies in England and their equivalents in Scotland, Wales and Northern Ireland: all social services departments; all district health authorities; all regional health authorities; all NHS trusts; all local education authorities; known deaf clubs and deaf voluntary organisations; all race equality councils; all community health councils; all family health service authorities; and all councils for voluntary services.

In addition, we contacted individuals and organisations known to us through personal contacts, snowballing and networking, and placed requests for information in both the minority ethnic and mainstream media. The media outlets used were *The Jang* (an Urdu language daily), the *Share Newsletter* (King's Fund), *LARRIE* bulletin (Local Authority Race Relations Information Exchange), *Community Care*, various deaf journals and the relevant Teletext pages on television.

A further effort at information gathering was made by sending out a video in BSL, requesting information, with Gohar Nisar presenting the questions and introducing co-authors Aliya Darr and Lesley Jones. The video request asked that information be provided either as written or video-recorded signed material, according to the language preference of the respondent. Requests for information were also made at Deaf conferences and rallies; and members of our Project Advisory Committee kept us informed of initiatives and contacts. We used this 'saturation' approach to ensure maximum coverage of initiatives.

Stage 3

Approximately 1,700 questionnaires were distributed in Stage 2. The responses which indicated any level of relevant activity were followed up by telephone (speech or text as appropriate) to obtain the relevant information. Where this was difficult we used faxed questions and responses. In this third stage we collected details about issues such as the focus, target groups, institutional base, user involvement and funding base of the identified initiatives. At the end of this stage, we had identified 104 initiatives of varying size, duration and focus. The material from these two stages forms the basis of Chapter 4 and informs the rest of the report. Details of individual projects are given in the *Directory of projects* (Darr et al, 1997).

Stage 4

In this stage, we conducted face-to-face interviews. In choosing initiatives for detailed interviews, we aimed to reflect the diversity of initiatives in terms of geographical distribution, target group (ethnicity, gender, Deaf or hard of hearing, etc), sectoral location (voluntary, statutory) and funding base (relatively secure initiatives as well as those with little secure funding). Where appropriate, we interviewed workers, users and line managers. Topic guides were used for loosely structured discussion. In total 85 interviews were conducted. Of these 45 were with 'providers' (workers, line managers, volunteers), 37 with users and 4 with researchers. Overall, 45 respondents were Deaf, hard of hearing or deafened and 40 were hearing. Most interviews were done individually but some were conducted as group interviews.

The four fieldwork stages were not as clear cut as they may appear. Through our own and the Project Advisory Committee's networks, we were able to identify and include new work throughout the life of the project.

A number of different approaches to communication were used with deaf respondents:

- a Deaf interviewer using British Sign Language with Deaf people;

- a hearing interviewer with a sign language interpreter with Deaf people;

- a hearing interviewer using sign-supported English;

- spoken English or other languages.

Hearing respondents were interviewed in English, Urdu, Punjabi, Gujarati and Bengali (last two with interpreters). The range of languages and approaches allowed respondents to use their preferred language.

All interviews with hearing respondents and with Deaf respondents using sign language interpreters were audio-recorded; those using BSL were video-recorded. The interviews in BSL and in spoken languages other than English were translated. Full transcripts were used for analysis, which focused on identifying themes and trends. In presenting the findings, we have located these in the context of services for minority ethnic people generally, and highlight many areas of similarity and difference.

The Advisory Committee

The Project Advisory Committee was made up of Deaf and hard of hearing people from minority ethnic communities, most working in relevant voluntary and statutory sectors or in the media. The Committee had a Deaf chairperson and communication was facilitated by sign language interpreters. Alex O'Neil represented the Joseph Rowntree Foundation. The Advisory Committee's role was crucial in guiding the project, helping with the focus, facilitating access to information and networks and bringing various initiatives to our attention and offering important moral support.